**STEP-BY-STEP**

# stained glass

A Complete Introduction to the Craft of Stained Glass

## By Erik Erikson

Conceived and edited by
**William and Shirley Sayles**

**GOLDEN PRESS · NEW YORK**
WESTERN PUBLISHING COMPANY, INC.
Racine, Wisconsin

# Foreword

This book invites you to look beyond technical pronouncements for the real meaning of stained glass, man's acknowledgment of the sacrament of light. While relating the practical requirements for mastering the craft of stained glass, the author reveals the interplay of art and mechanics, material and methods, to convey as much as anything else the epic human need for visual enlightment, for pure visual fulfillment. Think of what ordinary glass provides in this respect—it enables us to see as it admits light within and opens vistas beyond. And then think of the drama and beauty of stained glass as it intercepts light and calls attention to itself.

The current, wide-ranging experiment in the visual arts shows many examples of the application of stained glass, and, with new architecture, we are seeing a distinguished use of stained glass in buildings and residences as well as houses of worship. Outstanding examples of the art have been designed and executed by the author of this book.

Erik Erikson has been seriously involved for a number of years with sizes, shapes, and colors of pieces of glass. It is, apparently, a perfect role for him, as evidenced by his dedication to the work and his distinguished record of achievement in the profession. He has trained in this country and abroad to prepare himself for the demands he is now fulfilling as one of the top designers in this field, and as an exhibitor and teacher.

This book was written to present clearly the what and how of stained glass and to illuminate your individual quest for expression. It is a fundamental guide for the beginner, with a scope and detail that make it a valuable handbook for home use.

Francis Merritt
*Director, Haystack Mountain School of Crafts*
*Deer Isle, Maine*
*1974*

Library of Congress Catalog Card Number: 74-76678

# Contents

ACKNOWLEDGMENTS

In the course of preparing this book many crafts-men and craftswomen were asked for photographic examples of their work, and their cooperation was very gratifying—thanks go to them and also to the American Crafts Council for lending photographic materials from its collections. Thanks also go to Mr. Mel Greenland (The Greenland Studio), who gracious-ly allowed his studio to be used for many of the photographs shown here. Among those who have assisted in the preparation of this book, special thanks are due to Louis Mervar, photography, and Dagfinn Olsen, diagram inking.

# *Introduction*

To experience stained glass is to experience light as pure color. How and when the art of stained glass originated has not been completely traced. What is known is that glass itself was manufactured as early as 2500 B.C. in Egypt and the Tigris-Euphrates region. Glass-blowing, which to this day remains the principal method of making glass for stained glass windows, was developed about 100 B.C. Old accounts tell of stained glass church windows in 5th-century Rome and the Near East, and actual fragments of stained glass from the 8th century have been found. The oldest complete stained glass windows still in existence are in the Cathedral of Augsburg, Germany. These five windows, called the Prophets, are about six feet high and were made in the 11th century.

With the flourishing of Gothic architecture in the 12th and 13th centuries, the potential of stained glass was fully realized. Within barely 100 years, the Gothic method of construction had created soaring stone frameworks with immense sixty-foot apertures waiting to be filled with stained glass. Because it was not possible to make large sheets of glass, small pieces had to be assembled with leading to make larger units that would, in turn, be installed in the framework of the window. The completed windows depicted figures and stories of the Bible for a populace that could not read. The small stained glass pieces that comprised these windows caught and reflected light and sparkled in the sun like precious jewels.

In the middle of the 14th century a series of events occurred that marked the end of the pure Gothic tradition in stained glass. At that time the Cistercian Order of Catholic monks, opposed to the extravagance of color in pictorial stained glass windows, succeeded in inducing the use of plain white glass without figures. Subsequently, during the Protestant Reformation, many stained glass windows were actually ordered destroyed. In addition, the bubonic plague, coursing through Europe, resulted in the deaths of entire neighborhoods of glassworkers, together with their years of accumulated knowledge. Although it never truly disappeared, stained glass became known as the lost art. It was not until the 19th century that the Gothic revival stimulated a rediscovery of medieval approaches to the art of stained glass.

## STAINED GLASS TODAY

In this century, imitation has proceeded hand in hand with innovation, with the art of stained glass encompassing all historical periods as well as assimilating the ideas of 20th century painting. In the early 1900's the development of the international style in architecture and

Stained glass panel adds charm, color to kitchen. By Erik Erikson. Lead came, 16" sq. Collection, Margaret Hyatt.

(Facing page) Medieval lead came medallion window, approx. 25′ × 5′. In a church, southern France. Note repeat pattern of sections throughout, with painted pictorial detail within each section.

the existence of the Bauhaus in Germany gave rise to a new consideration of glass as an adjunct to architecture. In the 1950's stained glass commissions were given to many of the foremost European painters, and colored reproductions of their works in books and periodicals expanded an awareness of the glass medium.

Today there are many more people—amateurs as well as professionals—practicing stained glass than ever practiced the craft during the Middle Ages. No longer is the craft confined to a limited number of artisans and their apprentices, and no longer is the work produced by craftspeople confined to a very limited patronage. Stained glass can be found in homes, public buildings, office buildings, airports, and industries, as well as in houses of worship.

The basic technique of leading has changed little in the past 1,000 years—a remarkable indication of the lasting value of this dialogue between man and material. The one truly modern innovation is the use of adhesives such as epoxy and silicone. These broaden the possibilities of working with glass, but the fundamentals of light and color remain the same. Simplicity of procedure and the dramatic results produced make the craft an exciting and satisfying challenge that need not intimidate a beginner.

### THE GLASS ITSELF

The term "stained glass" might lead some to think that the glass is stained, or dyed, when in the sheet; in other words, that color is applied to a clear sheet and then fused to it in a kiln. Actually, however, color is principally the result of metal oxides added during the making of the glass.

To make a sheet of antique glass, a type often used in the stained glass process, the raw material is first heated in a pot; then the glass-blower dips a long tube into the molten batch, collects some at the end, and forms it into a bubble by blowing down the tube. As the bubble becomes elongated, it forms a hollow cylinder, which is cut down one side, while still hot, and allowed to settle on a flattening stone. There it opens to an uneven rectangular sheet of irregular thickness. In settling, the side of the glass that is resting on the stone will be marked with any particular texture that may be present there, while the upper surface of the glass will retain undulations from the blowing process.

### THIS BOOK

This book is a complete step-by-step guide to working with stained glass and is meant to start you on your way as surely and as simply as possible. It gives all the fundamentals for executing a large window in various techniques, but also includes small items that a beginner can complete over a weekend, such as a lapel pin, a belt buckle, a window hanging, a jewelry box, or a mirror frame. For

Detail. Contemporary leaded and painted window in the medieval tradition, by Joep Nicolas. One of a series of figure windows in a church, The Netherlands.

today, stained glass is used in myriad ways—in jewelry or for decoration, as shelving or to add color to a door, as a room divider or a wall panel. But without doubt, its most glorious use is still as a window or screen through which sunlight can stream.

Through this book it is hoped the novice will discover the romance of stained glass—its many tints, colors, and textures, and the ways in which it captures light. Vast possibilities exist for arranging, combining, and joining glass. Stained glass can be joined with a strong lead line or with no line at all. Glass pieces can be superimposed in a collage or relief, or faceted slab glass can be embedded in epoxy or plaster so that the sparkling glass chunks seem to float in space and shine like stars in the night.

The required tools and materials for accomplishing the techniques are basic, simple to use, and nominal in price. The book describes, step-by-step, all the phases of the stained glass process, including information on the glass itself, setting up a workshop, designing, pattern-making for cutting and arranging glass, the actual cutting of the glass, soldering, using epoxy and plaster, and surface treatments such as painting and etching.

In addition, six stained glass techniques—lead came, copper foil, slab glass, laminated glass, glass mosaics, and fused glass—along with variations, are discussed, and representative projects are given. Among these projects are stained glass lampshades that employ the lead came and copper foil techniques. The copper foil lampshades are included because of the influence and current popularity of the Tiffany style. The foil technique itself was developed at the turn of the century by Louis Comfort Tiffany, and was used mainly to fashion

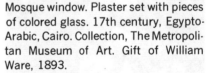

Mosque window. Plaster set with pieces of colored glass. 17th century, Egypto-Arabic, Cairo. Collection, The Metropolitan Museum of Art. Gift of William Ware, 1893.

Hanging lamp by Louis Comfort Tiffany, 1889. Copper foil, diameter 26". Collection, The Metropolitan Museum of Art. Gift of Mr. and Mrs. Douglas Williams in memory of Mr. and Mrs. Robert W. de Forest, 1969.

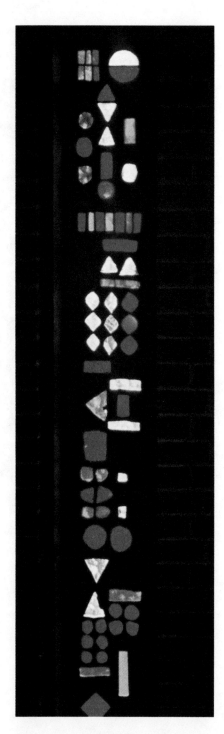

Slab glass window by Efrem Weitzman. Installation, Naurausham Presbyterian Church, Pearl River, N.Y.

what have come to be known as Tiffany lamps, delicate and lacy creations made in the Art Nouveau style of the day. The glass used for these lamps, as well as for windows and vases, was opalescent, handmade by the Tiffany studio.

## DESIGN

A unique part of this book is the section on design. There, the exercises that are given are based on combining geometric shapes and are geared toward working progressively. The initial simple unit, and those that follow, can be repeated in a variety of colors and subdivisions. Several units can be subsequently assembled into a larger, more complex whole, thus echoing the repetition of units seen in medieval windows. (It can then be seen that the medieval window is not as complex as it looks, but is made up of repeat modules.) In this way, a logical approach to design is established, and much of the initial perplexity that a beginner to design is apt to have is eliminated at the outset.

## FROM SHEET GLASS TO GRANULES

As you work with glass, save all your scraps, separating them in boxes according to color and type, for glass is usable in almost all sizes—from large sheets to tiny remnants. When a sheet of glass is cut into various sizes for a particular project, small pieces of glass are left over. These pieces, or scraps, are still valuable and form the basis for a number of techniques, as well as for small projects and the fabrication of glass jewelry. Larger-sized scraps can be used in several techniques, such as lamination or copper foil, or can be broken down into even finer pieces for application in the fused glass technique or as glass mosaics. Very small pieces approximate what is known as crushed glass—which ranges from small granules to powdered glass.

## REFERENCES

A glossary of terms follows on page 10. At the conclusion of the book is a list of suppliers for tools and materials, a list of books for further reading, and one of schools and workshops offering courses in stained glass.

(Facing page, top left) Copper foil oval sculptural form, approx. 14″ high. (Top right) Glass assemblage. Layered glass pieces set in deep frame 30″ square × 6″ deep. Installation, YWCA, Greenwich, Conn. (Bottom) Architecturally integrated leaded glass windows. Installation, Jack Lenor Larsen house.

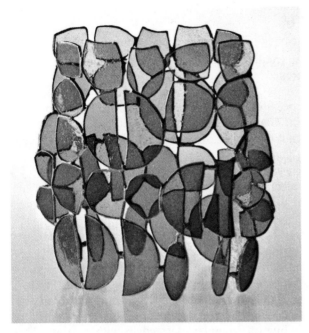

Glass assemblage by Fredrica H. Fields.

Sculptural form by Marlene Hoffman.

Lead came windows by Erik Erikson.

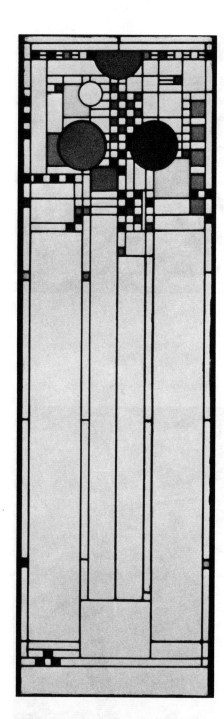

Framed leaded window by Frank Lloyd Wright. One of three in triptych, each 86¼″ × 28″ × 2″. Collection, The Metropolitan Museum of Art. Purchase, 1967.

# Glossary

Some of the most frequently used terms in this book are defined here for easy reference.

**Annealing**—the process of gradually cooling glass in a kiln to eliminate internal strain. Glass cooled too rapidly will crack.

**Antique glass**—handblown glass, so named to imply a resemblance to glass made in the past.

**Cartoon**—a full-size layout of a design sketch.

**Cathedral glass**—mechanically rolled and textured glass.

**Diffusion**—the spreading of light waves as they pass through translucent glass.

**Easel**—in stained glass, a sheet of plate glass on which to place cut glass pieces for viewing, selecting, or painting.

**Epoxy**—a plastic adhesive consisting of resin mixed with hardener.

**Firing**—heating glass in a kiln.

**Flux**—a substance, usually liquid, that cleans metals of oxides, thus allowing molten solder to flow and adhere.

**Groze**—to grind or bite off irregular glass edges with grozing pliers.

**Kiln**—a furnace in which high temperatures can be reached. Used for firing glass.

**Lead came**—a flexible lead strip, grooved to hold pieces of glass together.

**Opalescent glass**—a nontransparent glass having a milky, somewhat iridescent appearance, usually streaked with two or more colors.

**Patina**—a film formed by exposure or by treatment with acids. Used artistically to simulate age.

**Pattern**—a section of pattern paper cut to the exact shape of the glass. Used as guide for glass cutting.

**Refraction**—the bending of light waves as they pass through transparent glass.

**Sketch**—a scale drawing of a design.

**Tinning**—coating the copper tip of a soldering iron with solder.

**Translucent glass**—a semitransparent glass that allows passage of light but no clear view of the objects beyond.

**Transparent glass**—a glass that allows passage of light, clearly revealing the objects beyond.

**Note:** Clean all glass before cutting. Before using any of the techniques described, clean the glass again. Use alcohol, or ammonia and water, or detergent and warm water. Rinse and allow to dry. Once clean, hold glass only at the edges to prevent finger marks.

Window hanging by Erik Erikson.

Window hanging by Susan J. Greenbaum.

# *Lead Came*

In the lead came technique, which is commonly associated with medieval stained glass windows, flat pieces of glass are fitted into flexible lead came strips to form a composition. The came marks the lines of the design and holds the pieces of glass together. In forming a design, the came is cut where it meets another came. The intersecting joints are then soldered.

The total visual effect of a leaded piece is one of areas of color viewed against a dark filigree. As light filters through the glass, expanding and changing with the time and quality of the day, it silhouettes the leads and clearly outlines the design.

This technique is ideal for windows or window panels and is easily applied to three-dimensional pieces such as hanging lanterns, or the lampshade on page 50. The glass can be painted or etched, and glass jewels can be included in the design. Also, because came is pliable, panels can assume a variety of silhouettes, as seen in the window panel on page 76 or in the leaded window hanging by Erik Erikson shown above. This circular piece is 3′ in diameter and uses transparent glass in a variety of colors.

For this technique, see pages 44–51.

# *Copper Foil*

Copper foil was an innovation introduced at the turn of the century. Its development as a technique and its principal usage were in what have come to be known as Tiffany lamps, executed in the then prevailing Art Nouveau style. Because of its flexibility, its relative thinness, and the resultant narrow margins, copper foil was better suited to the small pieces of glass that made up the Tiffany lamps' intricate designs than was the traditional leading.

In this technique the edges of each piece of glass are wrapped with foil. Each foiled piece is then soldered to an adjacent one. Since small pieces of glass can be used, painting and other surface treatments are not necessary to achieve subtle nuances of color or delineation of form. Foil comes in wide rolls that are cut to size as needed, or in thin, precut rolls that are adhesive-backed.

Although the most popular use of this technique is in making lampshades, many other pieces can be fashioned using copper foil. Examples are shown throughout the book. The piece above by Susan J. Greenbaum, an 8″ square window hanging, uses four colors of opalescent glass.

For this technique, see pages 52–63.

Detail. Repeat panel by Erik Erikson.

Detail. Door panel by Harriet Hyams.

## *Slab Glass*

Slab glass is chunky—about ¾″ thick—and when embedded in plaster, concrete, or epoxy it forms a self-supporting unit that can be installed in a frame as a window panel, screen, or room divider.

In the techniques previously described, the metal holding the glass creates a linear pattern. In slab glass, the bonding agent poured around the glass creates areas that can be utilized in a more varied manner than lead or foil lines. The visual effect is created by the contrast of pieces of colored glass against a strong, black, silhouetted form.

The slab edges can be faceted, or chipped, thus adding a sparkling, jewel-like quality to the piece. The surface of the bonding agent can be textured with gravel or marble chips, or it can be molded.

Shown above is a detail of a repeat geometric panel by Erik Erikson. The varied design of slab chunks and epoxy textured with gravel is fixed in a metal grid. Note that although the glass pieces are irregularly shaped, they do not upset the total organization of the design.

For this technique, see pages 64–69.

## *Laminated Glass*

Epoxy is used in this technique to bind flat pieces of colored glass to a base of clear plate glass or to sandwich glass pieces together in a collage. A laminated glass design eliminates the black lines of a linear pattern and instead emphasizes color interaction and superimposition.

An exciting color mix takes place when the glass pieces are laminated to both sides of the plate glass so that colors overlap. The opportunity to mix colors is increased when two or more layers of glass are laminated to one side. Transparent glass is best for color mixing, and textured glass for added interest.

The cutting and fitting of the glass can be crucial; unless pieces are cut to fit exactly, irregular white spaces will occur between them. However, if the design allows for these spaces, cutting is simplified.

Room dividers, windows, and door panels are ideal projects for this technique. The above detail is from a door panel by Harriet Hyams. Lamination of glass pieces to plate glass doors is on one side only and the glass pieces are fitted closely together.

For this technique, see pages 70–72.

Transparent mosaic panel by Mariette Bevington.

Kiln-fired panel by Arthur Tieger.

## Glass Mosaics

The mosaic technique provides an ideal opportunity to utilize scraps of flat glass, whether purchased or left over from other projects. The glass pieces are used with an opaque epoxy grout, either with or without a base of clear plate glass. Design considerations should include the linear pattern created by the grout matrix. Spaces between the glass pieces can vary in width and direction, and the glass itself can be applied in a freehand style, cut to various shapes, or used in a gridwork design.

Window panels and table tops can be effectively made with this technique. Wall panels using opaque or translucent glass are also possible projects, since mosaics do not have to allow the passage of light. However, it is best to affix the glass pieces to a white, or nearly white, background so that the glass colors are clear and sparkling. Of course, with the use of a transparent backing such as plate glass, light filters through to radiate the colors.

In the panel by Mariette Bevington shown above (commissioned by Abraham & Straus Co.), note how well the design unifies glass pieces of different shapes.

For this technique, see page 72.

## Fused Glass

Both the laminated glass and the glass mosaic techniques rely on clear liquid epoxy as the bonding agent. In the fused glass technique, however, the material adheres to itself and/or to a plate glass backing, when heated to the point where the glass molecules combine. Such heating requires a kiln.

There are different stages of fused glass: fused just enough to bind glass to glass; fused until the edges are rounded off and become soft; and fused so that the different layers of glass sink to one level.

This technique relies on the tested compatibility of the glass used, or the acceptance of cracks that occur when incompatible types of glass are melted together. Very slow heating and very slow cooling are desirable procedures.

The resultant pieces may be arranged for their own design, or used in other techniques. Glass jewels are produced by this method.

The above example of kiln-fired glass is by Arthur Tieger. This 4″ square piece, in different colors, was made with opaque glass.

For this technique, see pages 74–75.

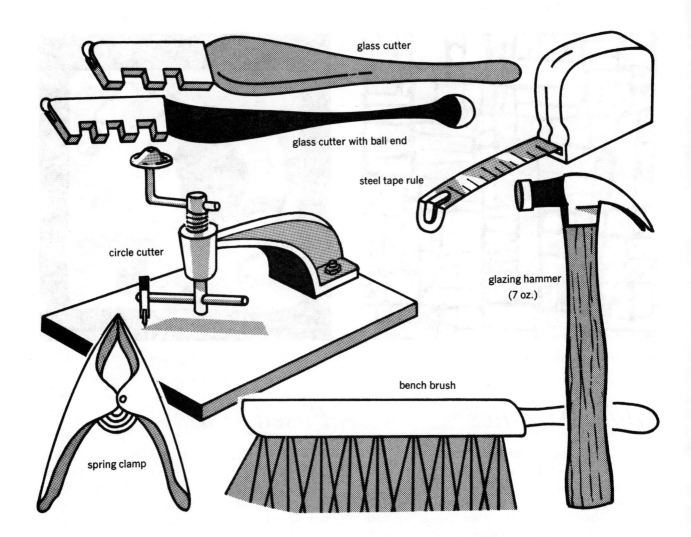

glass cutter

glass cutter with ball end

steel tape rule

circle cutter

glazing hammer (7 oz.)

bench brush

spring clamp

# Tools and Materials

The tools most generally used for stained glass are shown above. Other equipment, tools, and materials are described below and elsewhere in the book where they apply.

**Glass cutter** (Diamantor, Fletcher, or Red Devil)—scores glass so it can be snapped. Has a tiny steel wheel that rotates on a minute axle, and a metal, wooden, or plastic handle. Slots on shaft end may be used for chipping off small pieces of glass, but glass pliers or grozing pliers are preferable.

**Glass cutter with ball end**—steel wheel cutter, but with ball end (metal handle only) for tapping on underside of glass to help fracture score line.

**Circle cutter**—circles may be cut with a steel wheel cutter, but for perfect circles a circle cutter is necessary. One type (above) cuts circles ½″ to 5″ in diameter. Another type for larger circles (not shown) has a suction cup that affixes to glass sheet.

**Spring clamp**—holds wooden or metal straightedge used in scoring straight lines in large sheets of glass. Other assorted uses.

**Steel tape rule**—for measuring purposes. Folding wood rule may also be used.

**Bench brush**—used constantly during cutting process to sweep small chips of glass from workbench.

**Tacking or glazing hammer**—used during lead came process and to tack paper patterns.

**Glass pliers**—shaped to snap off pieces of glass too small to grasp with hands, as well as any tiny chips

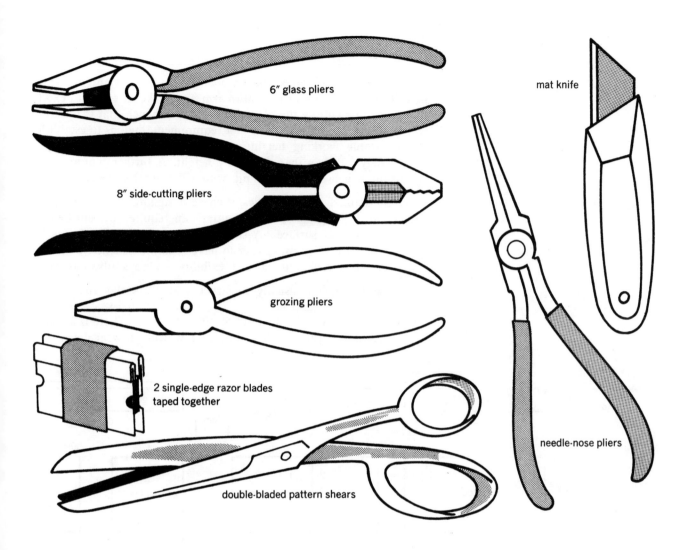

6″ glass pliers

8″ side-cutting pliers

grozing pliers

2 single-edge razor blades taped together

double-bladed pattern shears

mat knife

needle-nose pliers

on glass edge. Also for cutting deep curves. 6″ pliers recommended.

**Grozing pliers**—to groze, or trim away, jagged glass edges and to shape glass pieces for better fitting.

**Side-cutting pliers**—to cut copper wire for use as loops and to stretch lead came. Other assorted uses.

**Needle-nose pliers**—for straightening came flanges, twisting copper wire for loops, and other uses.

**Mat knife**—various cutting purposes. X-Acto knife may also be used.

**Double-bladed pattern shears**—specifically for lead came patterns. Center blade cuts away width of paper equal to heart of came. Shears come in two sizes. Sizes refer to thickness of center blade (1.5 mm. recommended). Single-edge razor blades may be used instead.

**Single-edge razor blades**—for general cutting purposes and as substitute for shears. For the latter, make double-edged cutter by taping two blades together with $1/16''$ thick piece of cardboard between.

**MATERIALS AND OTHER EQUIPMENT.** 45° **triangle, roofing square,** and **straightedge**—for aligning. **Masking tape**—for general taping. **Heavy tracing paper** or **tracing cloth** (plastic sheeting)—for copying purposes. **Brown wrapping paper**—used for assembly diagram in designing and to cover work surfaces (30 lb. Kraft paper used professionally). **Oak tag paper**—lightweight cardboard used as cutting pattern for design (90 lb. Kraft paper used professionally). **Homasote**—lightweight composition board used to cover workbench and to provide cutting surface.

# *Workshop*

For the most part stained glass work is done while standing. This permits a freer action of the entire arm and makes it easier to exert pressure while cutting the glass. Working at a bench that is too low will guarantee a backache. The first requirement, then, is to establish a comfortable working height. A good workbench height is approximately 33″ less than full body height. A further requirement is that the bench be sturdily built, with a flat, level surface.

Different stained glass activities, such as designing, cutting, glazing (process of leading glass), or cementing can require different bench heights as well as surfaces. A small board could be used for each activity, but it is obviously easier to have separate benches. Benches could also have rollers attached. Flexibility is always advantageous.

The glazing bench is usually constructed of 2″ × 4″s and is put together with bolts and lag bolts. The most desirable wood for the top of the bench is 2″ × 8″ or 2″ × 10″ solid stock. There is a good deal of hammering in the glazing process, which will wear down the

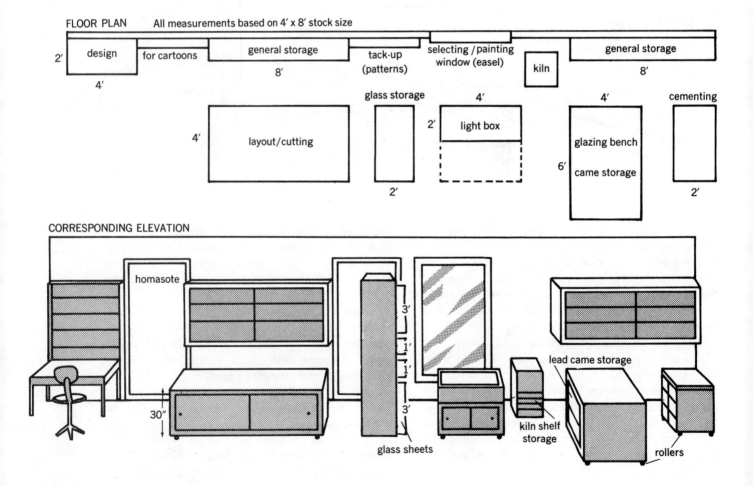

FLOOR PLAN    All measurements based on 4′ x 8′ stock size

CORRESPONDING ELEVATION

wood, but this surface can be made level again with a belt or disc sander. You can also use 1″ × 10″ solid stock and place it over a sheet of ¾″ plywood. Change the stock as it wears down. Plywood will not do as a top surface, since it splinters easily when hammered.

**Storage.** As shown on facing page, the spaces beneath the workbenches can be designed to accommodate various tools and materials. Lead came purchased from a supplier comes in boxes slightly more than 6′ long. These can be stored quite readily beneath the benches. A general rule regarding lead came is to handle it as little as possible before using and to stretch it immediately prior to use. There are also storage racks for the glass—large racks for large pieces and successively smaller ones for those pieces that have been cut down.

## LIGHT BOXES

Although colored glass is most visually exciting when viewed against variable natural daylight, it is not practical to have to depend solely on that light source. A light box, therefore, is of great value in the stained glass process. Its uses are many. It can be used in selecting glass colors and in visualizing the relationship of one color glass to another, but ideally only when the final result is to be viewed against artificial light. It is also useful when tracing designs and when painting on glass.

Portable light boxes are available from art suppliers, but you can easily make your own. The one shown can be set into a specially-made table on rollers or incorporated into a workbench. Set flush with the surface of the workbench or table. Wiring is not difficult; ventilation is desirable. Construct a box 8″ deep. Gauge the width and length in accordance with the size of the fluorescent light tubes that are to be used. Paint the inside of the box white for a reflective surface. Fasten two or more fluorescent tubes to the bottom, approximately 6″ from the front and back of the box, and 6″ apart. Top box with ¼″ frosted glass, shiny side up. Drill holes for ventilation. Fluorescent light is preferred to incandescent light, as it most closely approximates natural daylight.

## SAFETY

The following common sense precautions will probably occur to anyone working with glass: Do not work where food is prepared or eaten. Do not wear open-toed shoes or go barefoot. Keep hands away from mouth and wash them well after working. Handle a sheet of glass with both hands and do not attempt to pick it up by one corner. Sweep floor at intervals. Use bench brush constantly on workbench to sweep away chips of glass. Keep a first-aid kit handy.

Store any liquid substances that could in any way be regarded as combustible in a fireproof cabinet. Dispose of any oily rags right away; if not possible to do so, place in a small metal can with a lid.

**Light box.** Extremely valuable for tracing, painting, selecting glass colors, and other uses. Commercially available.

LIGHT BOX CONSTRUCTION

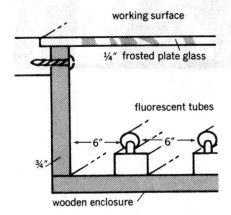

working surface

¼″ frosted plate glass

fluorescent tubes

6″  6″

¾″

wooden enclosure

**Homemade light box.** Easily constructed, it can be set into a table made especially for it, or incorporated into a workbench. Allow sufficient height to permit proper diffusion of light.

# Glass

There are two basic types of glass used in the stained glass process—handblown and machine-made. Handblown glass is blown with a blowpipe, then cut and allowed to flatten out, or blown in textured molds. Machine-made glass is mechanically rolled, poured in molds, or pressed in molds. The irregular texture and thickness of handblown glass is more varied in coloration and sparkle than machine-made glass, which has a more or less uniform texture and thickness and a rolled pattern that causes light to diffuse.

**HANDBLOWN GLASS. Antique.** Made mostly in Germany, France, and England, it is so named to imply a resemblance to glass made in the past. German and French glass have the same approximate sheet size (30″ × 24″) and vary in thickness within each sheet; fine distinctions can be made as to coloration and texture. English glass, usually the most expensive, is smaller (about 16″ × 20″), generally thicker, and distinguished by an elegant surface texture and very subtle color variations. Blenko, the sole American antique glass, is different from the others, with perhaps greater variation of thickness in a single sheet and an almost pebbly texture that is the result of being blown in a mold.

**Pot Metal, Streaky, Flashed.** All handblown glass is pot metal—glass colored in the pot while molten. However, current usage of the term indicates glass of a single color throughout, unlike streaky which is a blend of more than one color, or flashed, a thin layer of deeply colored glass "flashed" on a thick base of clear or lightly tinted glass. Striking effects can be achieved by etching or engraving the flashed layer. *Opaline,* flashed with opal, deserves special mention. Mainly from West Germany, it is not to be confused with opalescent, a machine-rolled glass, although the same mineral, opal, is used to produce its iridescent surface reflections and muted color.

**Reamy, Seedy, Crackle.** All refer to texture in or on the glass. Reamy (or Danziger) has a swirling surface undulation; seedy is sprinkled with minute bubbles throughout. The webbed pattern of crackle is a result of the glass being dipped in water during the blowing process.

**Rondel.** A circle of glass made by spinning a blown bubble on a punty rod until it opens into a flat disc. Characteristic of the rondel is the knobby mark in its center where the rod has been "cracked off." Machine-pressed rondels are identified by their centers which are not as sharp-pointed as those of the handblown rondels. Rondels come in various colors and sizes and can be cut or used as they are.

**MACHINE-MADE GLASS. Cathedral.** A domestic glass in greater supply that costs less than handblown. Sheets as large as 11′ × 5′ are produced in a variety of textures, some designated "antique" or "semi-antique." The designations refer to patterns impressed on the glass by metal rollers and carry names such as oceanic, ripple, moss, granite, hammered, figure C, Florentine, and Flemish.

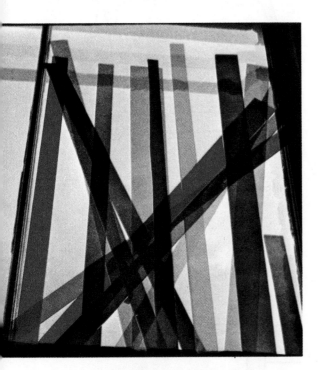

Assorted strips of antique handblown glass from Europe, set against natural light for color selecting.

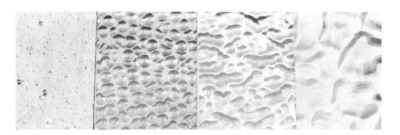

Samples of machine-made glass. Textures and patterns are impressed on glass by mechanical rollers.

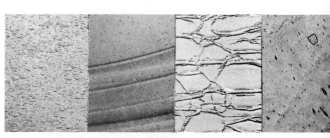

Samples of hand blown glass textured by hand tooling and by addition of chemicals while glass is in molten state.

**Opalescent.** A near-opaque glass with an iridescent color quality. It is commonly associated with Tiffany stained glass work, although there is a vast difference between the machine-rolled opalescent of today and the handmade opalescent produced by Tiffany.

**Slab and Pressed.** Glass, once it is poured into a mold, can be cast (allowed to harden without pressure) or pressed (formed under pressure). Slabs, or dalles, thick glass 8″ × 12″ × ¾″, are cast in open molds. Pressed glass, usually small geometric shapes impressed with designs, is used for ornament in lamps, borders, and windows.

The foregoing describes the principal glasses used in the stained glass process. However, all glass is potentially usable, if appropriate to the design. "Commercial" glass, including clear, patterned, beaded, and even mirror glass, may be used. Bottle bottoms are usable, as are pieces from old glass panels found in secondhand stores. It is best not to discount any glass, but to make an educated choice based on the potentialities and character of the glass available.

**Selecting glass.** The choice of one type of glass over another is based on personal preference as well as practical considerations such as color, texture, degree of opacity, quality of refraction, ease of cutting, and reaction to firing if the glass is to be painted. Glass to be viewed close up suggests the use of more textural variation than does glass to be viewed from a distance, where such texture would be less important. Glass rolled with an allover pattern is, on the whole, more translucent (and the light that shines through more diffused) than handblown glass, which is transparent but irregular because of texturing.

A general rule is to select glass against that light which most closely approximates the light against which the completed piece will be seen. Once a project is established, the usual procedure is to go to a glass house or local dealer, or to order by mail. Glass is sold in sheets of various sizes or in remnants by weight. Buying remnants is a practical step for the beginner both because of cost and because of the likelihood that there will be a greater variety of glass from which to choose. Save your scraps when cutting sheet glass; they can be used in various techniques.

Pressed glass assortment in a variety of colors. These "jewels" can be used in windows and pieces for the home.

BASIC LEAD CAME SHAPES

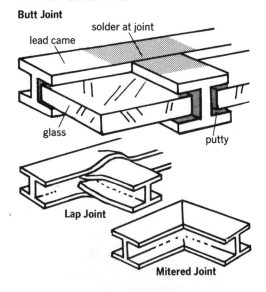

METHOD FOR JOINING

**Butt Joint**

**Lap Joint**

**Mitered Joint**

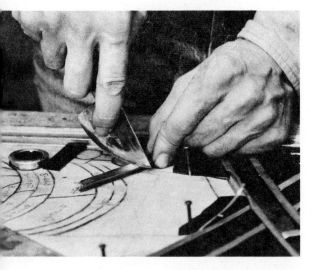

Cutting lead came for joining. Came and glass fitted over assembly diagram and secured with nails and lathing.

# Basic Processes

Each stained glass technique demonstrates a means by which pieces of glass are held together to be viewed against light. Lengths of lead came are used in one instance, strips of copper foil in another, a thick matrix of epoxy, concrete, or plaster in still another. Glass pieces can also be fused to a transparent backing and to each other. Accordingly, this section deals with the various means of joining the glass and of providing structural support for the piece.

## LEAD CAME

In the lead came technique, pieces of colored glass are held together by means of lead came strips. The came, a soft, flexible material that conforms easily to the shape of the glass, comes in lengths of approximately 6′. When seen in cross section, flat came resembles the letter H laid on its side. It has a crossbar down its middle, with two channels on either side. This crossbar, or heart, is approximately $1/16$″ thick and serves to separate from each other the pieces of glass that are fitted under the lip, or flange, of the came.

Lead came is available in a variety of shapes and widths. The most generally used widths are $3/16$″, $1/4$″, $5/16$″, $3/8$″, $1/2$″, $5/8$″, $3/4$″, 1″, and $1\frac{1}{2}$″. Flat came and half-round came are the most commonly used shapes. These names refer to the shape of the came seen in cross section. There are also special-purpose cames—such as high-heart, off-heart, and U channel. The latter has only one channel and may be used to give a finished appearance to the outside edges of a stained glass piece that is not designed to be set into a molding. For your beginning work, it is suggested that you use $3/8$″ or $1/4$″ flat lead came.

**Lap and butt joints.** During the process of fitting lead came and glass in accordance with a predetermined design, the came is cut wherever it meets another came, either at an angle or where the two cames cross. And where the lengths meet they are joined in either a lap joint or a butt joint. The butt joint can be straight or mitered, depending on how the cames meet. Solder is subsequently melted onto these joints with a hot soldering iron to bind one leaded piece of glass to another.

**Lap joint** (for flat came only; half-round came cannot be joined in this manner). This is a strong, clean joint if done well. The end of one came strip is slipped under the top and bottom flanges of the other by first flaring the overlapping came at the joint (see diagram). Since this sometimes results in a very tight fit, the came that is to be slipped under the flanges must be carefully hammered flat.

**Butt joint** (for both flat and half-round came). The came is cut to meet edge to edge. This means cutting back the width of the flange, in between the glass pieces, where one came meets the other. The came must be carefully cut on the vertical for a straight butt (see diagram), or a gap will result, requiring patching. The lead is cut to meet on the diagonal for a mitered butt joint (see diagram).

## COPPER FOIL

Copper foil resembles lead came in its finished, soldered appearance, but because of its pliability and resultant thin line, it is better suited than the came to small pieces of glass. The individually wrapped pieces can also be applied to curved surfaces, such as lampshades. Copper foil is available in wide rolls sold by the pound and in narrow rolls that are adhesive-backed.

The wide rolls come 6″ and 12″ wide and in thicknesses ranging from .005″ for heavy work to .001″ for finer wrapping. In order to have the widths required for the work at hand, strips are cut from these rolls prior to use. Just cut off a length from the roll and fold it over into three or four layers (see diagram, page 52). Mark off the widths by scoring the foil, then cut along the score lines for the strips. Since this foil is sold by weight and in bulk, it is less expensive in the long run than the adhesive-backed foil, but the latter is precut for use and, therefore, a great timesaver.

Adhesive-backed foil is available in rolls ³/₁₆″, ¼″, or ⅜″ wide and 36 yards long. This foil is a boon to the beginner because of its convenience. It is necessary only to unroll enough foil to rim each piece of glass, allowing for an overlap of about ¼″ where the two ends meet. The adhesive coating on the back of the foil is protected by a strip of paper, which is peeled away as the foil is used.

After a foil length has been completely wrapped around the edges of a piece of glass, it is pressed tightly down onto the surfaces to form neat margins. The end effect is that of a minute U channel. The thickness of the glass will determine the width of the copper foil used; the advantage of working with a narrow width is that there will be a narrower margin on the glass and, therefore, a thinner line.

When all the pieces of glass have been foiled, each piece is then soldered to an adjacent one (see photo). Unlike lead came, which is soldered just at the joints, where came meets came, the foil is completely coated with solder, with the result that no foil remains visible (see diagram). It is this complete coating with solder that gives foil its visual resemblance to lead came.

## EPOXY

The techniques in this book that use epoxy are slab glass, laminated glass, crushed glass, and glass mosaics. Epoxy is essentially a clear bonding agent, but is also available with fillers of various colors—white, gray, brown, and black—that extend and opacify the substance. The epoxy comes in two parts—a resin and a catalytic hardener—and can be purchased in tubes at dime stores, in tubes and containers at hardware stores, or in larger quantities through suppliers. Mix carefully according to manufacturer's directions. Work

COPPER FOIL TECHNIQUE

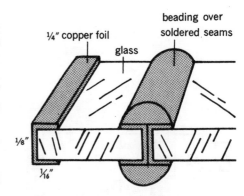

Detail showing relationship of glass to copper foil to solder. Note that entire foiled surface is soldered.

Soldering foiled seams. Note positions of solder and soldering iron. A rectangular piece is held by lathing.

in a dust-free room with good ventilation, as epoxy fumes are noxious. Wear rubber gloves to protect your hands from any irritation.

**Slab glass usage.** In this procedure, slab glass pieces are arranged, according to design, within a temporary frame, and liquid epoxy or concrete is poured around them. The hardened panel is then installed in an exterior architectural opening. If the piece is to be used for interior purposes, plaster can be the matrix.

The principal advantage of using epoxy over either plaster or concrete is that epoxy bonds to the glass and automatically weatherproofs the panel. This is because the coefficients of slab glass and epoxy are very similar, which simply means that the two materials expand and contract at a similar rate and to a similar degree with temperature changes. This is not so with concrete and glass, and one of the difficulties with this combination is weatherproofing. The second advantage of using epoxy is weight. A finished epoxied panel weighs about one-fifth as much as a comparable concrete panel, which makes installation understandably less difficult.

The epoxy in an epoxied panel is only ½″ to ⅝″ thick as compared to the ¾″ thickness of plaster or concrete, which is poured flush with the glass. Epoxy thickness is shown in diagram at left. The exact amount of epoxy mixture needed cannot be accurately determined, as it is relative to the amount of glass used, but less than a quart is usually required for each square foot of panel. Prepare in two separate mixings as two pourings are required. The proportion of resin to hardener is very important, as is room temperature. Both influence the setting and curing of epoxy. As shown in the photo at left, epoxy is poured through a paper funnel.

**Laminated glass usage.** Laminated glass is essentially flat pieces of colored, textured glass sandwiched together with crystal clear epoxy on a sheet of clear plate glass. Although the clear epoxies have improved with the years, they still have a tendency to turn yellow with time, due to ultraviolet radiation. For the most part, however, this yellowing is not discernible and presents no problem.

### KILN-FIRING

The firing and annealing information given here applies to the fusing technique (fusing glass pieces together) and to the painting technique (fusing paint to stained glass).

**Kiln.** For the home craftsperson, small electric kilns of the kind that are usually used for firing enamels or ceramics are available. These kilns run on regular house current. There are also front-loading flatbed kilns that are made especially for fusing glass and have a number of removable shelves made of steel or firebrick. These kilns are usually electric, but gas kilns are also available that give superlative results. Small kilns can be operated on a standard current of 110 volts; larger ones generally require a 220-volt line but this varies with the brand.

SLAB GLASS TECHNIQUE

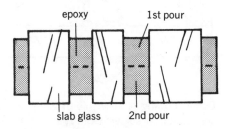

Detail showing relationship of slab glass to epoxy matrix. Piece is turned over for second pouring after first has set.

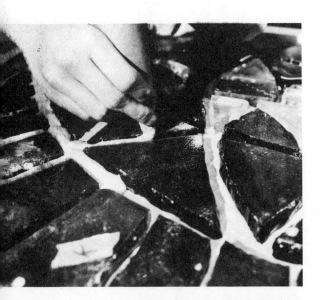

Pouring epoxy between pieces of slab glass with a paper funnel onto bed of fine sand.

A small kiln limits the size of the pieces that can be fused, but for initial purposes this should not be a disadvantage. The most practical kiln is one that has an insulated front-loading door that opens downward or to either side. The door must function quickly since any prolonged opening to observe the glass during firing will create an appreciable heat loss. The beginner can also fire in a top-loading kiln (see photo). In either a front-loading or top-loading kiln, the walls should be thick enough for proper annealing (the gradual cooling of glass to remove internal strain).

The kiln you purchase will undoubtedly come with firing instructions. However, since firing can vary from kiln to kiln, it is recommended that you fire a series of tests before firing a designed piece. Such tests will help familiarize you with the performance of the kiln, the fusing temperatures of different types of glass, and the rate and amount of cooling necessary to anneal glass so that it will not crack.

**Firing.** To prevent the fusion of glass pieces to the kiln shelf, coat the shelf with a powdered substance called kiln wash. Mix with water and brush on. Prior to placing the glass piece on the shelf, sift the kiln wash powder directly onto the shelf. This coat will minimize texture picked up on the fused piece during firing. Carefully place the glass piece on the shelf and insert both into the kiln.

Begin firing with the kiln door slightly open so that residual gasses can escape, moisture can evaporate, and glass can heat gradually. If heated too rapidly, the glass will crack. At 500° F. close the door. At 1000° F. the surface of the glass will turn a glossy orange-red, and its edges will start to round off. These temperatures are approximate. Without testing, it is difficult to predict the exact temperature at which any one glass will fuse. Generally, however, it is about 1300° F. for antique glass to about 1400° F. for machine-made glass. In fusing paint to glass, the temperature is usually about 1100° F.

Most kilns have a pyrometer (a gauge that indicates degree of heat within a kiln chamber), but it will probably not be sufficiently sensitive to gauge the one or two degrees in temperature (and seconds in time) between fusing and melting temperatures. Hence, it is necessary to gauge the final critical degrees with your eye. If it is not possible to observe the glass through the peephole in the kiln, you will have to open the door. So as not to lose heat, open it *slightly* and look in for *just an instant* from a safe distance.

**Annealing.** As defined previously, annealing is the gradual cooling of the glass to eliminate internal strain; glass too rapidly cooled will crack. Sometimes cracking can occur months later. Therefore, for proper annealing of the glass, switch the kiln off when the optimum fusing stage is reached. So that the glass does not overfire, it may be necessary to open the door slightly for about half a minute to keep the temperature from rising further. Then close the door and allow the kiln to cool gradually. (Twelve hours is not too long for glass to cool, even in a small kiln.)

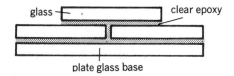

**Laminated glass.** Detail of two layers of glass sandwiched by epoxy on clear base.

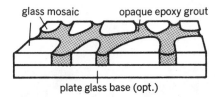

**Glass mosaics.** Detail showing small pieces of glass in opaque grout matrix.

**Fused glass.** Detail showing three progressive results of fusing glass in kiln.

Small panel of colored glass on glass base being fused in a top-loading electric kiln.

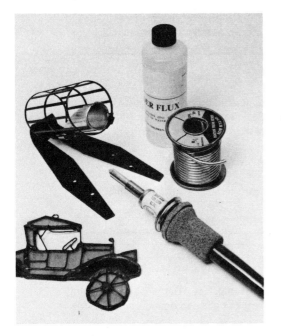

**Soldering setup.** Shown are lightweight pencil iron with holder, soldering flux, and ⅛″ wire solder on spool.

# *Soldering*

Leaded or foiled pieces of glass are bonded permanently together by melting solder on the metal with a hot soldering iron. The solder, which comes in ⅛″ wire, is an alloy of tin and lead and is designated by the ratio of one to the other. Since 60/40 solder is the easiest flowing, it is used the most.

**Tools and materials:** small hammer, brass brush or grade 0 steel wool, flux, solder, soldering iron, sponge.

**Flux.** Cleans came and foil, prevents oxidation, and causes solder to flow. Applied prior to soldering. Oleic acid is used for lead came; zinc chloride or oleic acid for copper foil. It is best to avoid acid core solder for came, as it leaves a corrosive residue.

**Soldering irons.** Available in different weights and wattages, with either copper or ironclad plug tips of various shapes and sizes. Use whatever you find appropriate for the work at hand. Ironclad tips come pretinned (tinning is necessary for proper soldering) and do not pit, erode, or scale. Their extra cost is made up for by the time and bother of repeated filing, tip changes, and tinning necessary with copper tips. If your iron has a screw-in tip, remove it from the iron when work is done so it will not "freeze" in place.

Unless the iron is hot enough, solder will not flow. Control heat by turning iron on and off. As irons do not come with switches, either add one or set up a hanging socket above workbench with a small red bulb and pull chain (bulb tells you if iron is on or off). Or use a rheostat, a device that controls wattage. Just set dial for amount of heat required and work continuously without disconnecting iron.

The life of a tip is extended by keeping it clean and well-tinned. Wipe it across a wet cellulose sponge as you work to remove flux and solder residue (see diagram, facing page). Do not wipe on dry rag or abrasive surface. Rinse sponge in clear water when work is done.

SOLDERING IRON

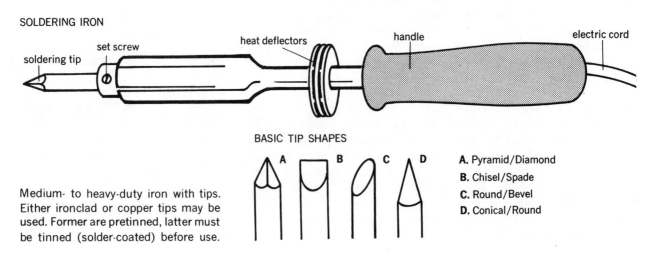

soldering tip · set screw · heat deflectors · handle · electric cord

Medium- to heavy-duty iron with tips. Either ironclad or copper tips may be used. Former are pretinned, latter must be tinned (solder-coated) before use.

BASIC TIP SHAPES

A B C D

**A.** Pyramid/Diamond
**B.** Chisel/Spade
**C.** Round/Bevel
**D.** Conical/Round

**Tinning** (applying a coat of solder to tip). Repeated heating and soldering cause copper tips to scale and corrode, making retinning necessary. File tip to clean it, then heat, and rub it on either a block of rosin or sal ammoniac. Coat by dipping into solder in an inverted jar lid. Tin ironclad tips in the same way, but *do not file.*

## SOLDERING LEAD CAME

**1.** Lightly tap each lead joint (if flat came) with a small hammer, so that it is as flat as possible for soldering. With a wire brush or steel wool, clean joints of lead oxide. Dirt impedes solder flow. With a square-tipped brush, dab flux on joints. Not much is needed.

**2.** Heat iron. Lay end of 60/40 solder on joint. Press with hot tip to melt solder and bridge the two lengths to be joined. Solder should flow wherever flux has been applied. Lift iron and observe results. A beginner tends to apply too much solder and, in attempting to smooth the excess, hold the iron on the joint too long. The result is melted came (concentrating heat in one place can also cause glass to crack). At a certain temperature below flowing point, solder follows a hot iron. This knowledge is helpful in removing excess solder.

**3.** Completely solder one side, then wipe excess flux off glass with a rag. Do not wait, as residue is difficult to remove. Turn work over (see page 49) and repeat soldering process.

## SOLDERING COPPER FOIL

**1.** Heat iron. Make sure foil is pressed tightly down. Place glass pieces on assembly diagram. Dab foil at intersections with zinc chloride or oleic acid flux, being careful not to move pieces. Tack pieces with 60/40 solder. Tack soldering holds pieces together for permanent soldering. If iron is very hot, you can use acid-core solder (for *tacking only*), which eliminates need for flux and the possibility of fluxing brush moving pieces out of position. If you use acid-core solder, clean very well.

**2.** Turn work to back. Flux entire copper surface. Touch end of 60/40 solder to foil. Draw hot tip along so that solder flows. No copper should remain visible. If iron gets too hot, or you dally in your work, the solder will slip through to front of piece. An alternate method is to use 40/60 or 50/50 solder. Their higher melting points will inhibit slippage and will also make the back of the piece sturdier. Then use 60/40 on the front.

**3.** Turn to front. If necessary, flatten tacking solder with hot iron. Flux, then solder with 60/40, working quickly so that solder does not overheat and slip through seams. Then pick up piece and coat edges, using the remaining excess flux and solder. Return to front, flux, then float a second coat of solder on for a rounded, beaded, finished look. Use an iron that is not too hot and work quickly.

**4.** Wash piece gently and thoroughly with soap and water, if zinc chloride was used. If oleic acid was used, see pages 47–49 for cleaning.

Soldering tinned copper wire around foiled piece to add strength to edges.

TO CLEAN TIP

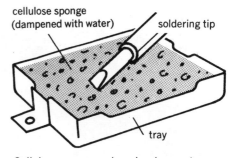

Cellulose sponge in aluminum tray. Iron tip is wiped on damp sponge during soldering to keep it clean. Tray holds reservoir of water.

# Surface Treatments

### PAINTING

The purpose of painting on glass is to obtain detailed imagery that cannot be achieved in any other way and to modify the amount of light coming through the glass. Painting on translucent refractive glass is in many ways quite the opposite of painting on an opaque

**1.** Tracing linear design on glass, working over light box. Note hand rest (easily constructed from wood).

**2.** Mixing matt color, gum arabic, and water together on glass palette with palette knife.

**3.** (Above) Applying matt by laying it down in successive strokes. **4.** (Right) Completed fired piece. Brushes were used to apply and remove matt. Note toning.

reflective surface, such as canvas. Light shining through the glass, rather than light bouncing off the surface, makes the image visible. Painting on glass also differs in that paint is applied and then partially removed in order to expose the underlying surface of the glass and to create shaded areas and tones.

Techniques for painting on glass involve both the application of paint and its removal. Three are offered here. For the most part painting consists of tracing (painting the main lines of the design) and matting (coating the surface with paint, then partially removing it by brushing, stippling, combing, scraping, or other means).

Matt paint is more translucent when fired than tracing paint. It is brushed on evenly over the entire surface. A blender brush is then whisked very lightly back and forth over the wet matt (usually in a direction that crosses matting strokes at right angles) to smooth it so that no streaks are apparent. The purpose of the matt is to give shaded areas to the tracing design and tones to the colored glass.

Paint itself is made up of pigment (a colorant in powdered form), a binder to hold it together and adhere it to the glass, and a vehicle to make it spreadable. An important aspect of glass painting is the application of several layers without disturbing the ones underneath. Accordingly, the substances (binders and vehicles) mixed with the pigments must be considered in terms of their reaction to each other. Some of the substances used are gum arabic, kerosene, and isopropyl alcohol. An alcohol or kerosene matt, for instance, can be applied on top of a dried gum and water matt without loosening it, provided the brushing action is competently done.

The principal pigments are tracing black, umber brown, bistre brown, and gray-green grisaille. The pigment is impermanent until fired. Therefore the substances used with the pigments must also be considered in terms of their reaction to heat.

**Waxing up on a glass easel.** Before removing matt, position glass pieces on an easel (page 35) and adhere with heated wax (usually one part beeswax to two parts rosin). Apply with a large eyedropper at those points where lead joints will be soldered. The temperature of the wax is critical: too hot, and it will run; too cold, and it will not flow and adhere. Take care not to drip wax onto the painted surface, as this will mean redoing the piece. Complete waxing up and set easel against natural light. Remove matt where desired. When finished, chip off wax.

Some glass artisans prefer removing the matt while working over a light box, then waxing up on an easel to observe the total effect and to add deep toning or strong shadowing.

(Right) "Naphtali," by Ahron Elvaiah. One of twelve leaded windows representing the twelve tribes of Israel. Installed, Fresh Meadows Jewish Center, Flushing, N.Y.

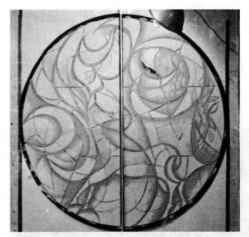

Cartoon. Charcoal on brown paper.

Piece painted while waxed up on easel.

Completed leaded window. Diameter 6'.

(Above) "A Saint Bishop" and detail. Early stained glass painted window. Tonality achieved by fine linear brushwork as much as by application of matt. 42½" × 21¾". Collection, Worcester Art Museum, Worcester, Mass.

(Left) "Crucifixion," by Erik Erikson. Leaded panel painted on clear glass. Undermatted, traced over, then overmatted, to simulate patina.

(Below) Detail. An example of a stained glass window showing use of stenciling to duplicate toning, in a floral motif.

**KEY TO PAINTING TOOLS**

1. Palette knives
2. Ox hair tracing brush
3. Camel hair matting brush
4. Badger hair blender
5. Bamboo scratching tool
6. Metal scratching comb
7. Pig bristle brushes or matt removers
8. Flat stencil brush or matt remover
9. Pig bristle stippler

The beginner, however, is advised to commence piece by piece, working flat over a light box. Working on an easel produces a more unified result when a large panel is being made and design lines must be carried from one section to another. But, at the beginning, you will probably be working on small pieces and most likely will not have so many pieces that painting on an easel would be required.

**Techniques.** In Technique **1** the traced lines are tack fired, which means fired at 900° F. in kiln. At this temperature paint does not permanently fuse to glass, but is held sufficiently through application of matt and its subsequent removal. Tack firing is not required in Techniques **2** or **3**. Firing information is on page 23.

**1.** (A simple basic procedure; refer to photos on page 26.) Grind the tracing color with gum arabic and water, using a palette knife on a plate glass palette. Add as little gum as possible (gum helps pigment adhere to glass, but too much will cause paint to blister or fry in firing). With the tracing color, trace linear design on glass (photo 1), then tack fire. Usually the cartoon is placed on the light box, under the glass, so design lines can be easily followed.

Grind matt color with gum arabic and water (photo 2) and apply with camel hair brush (photo 3). Blend immediately, while still wet, with a badger hair brush blender. Sometimes stippling is also done. Allow piece to dry. Then, with brush or scratching tool, remove matt where you want the color of the glass to show through. This is always an exciting experience. Fire completed piece (photo 4). Cover any leftover paint with plastic or store in jar. Add more water before using again.

**2.** Matt entire piece with umber brown ground in water and gum arabic. Scratch through matt with pointed stick to delineate design; further remove paint with a dry bristle brush. Fire the result. Note: Texturing can be obtained by dribbling water on dried gum matt. When dry, rub surface with fingers. Further brushing is possible.

STENCIL TECHNIQUE

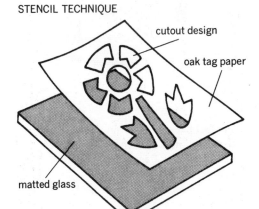

**A.** Laying stencil on matted glass.

**B.** Stenciled result, ready for firing.

A stencil can be used to help control design when removing matt from desired areas.

**3.** Matt entire piece with umber brown ground in water and gum arabic. Using tracing black (ground in water with gum), apply lines with tracing brush. As you will not be able to see through glass to trace from cartoon, your line will have to be spontaneous. Remove matt where desired to get an interesting play between the line and the matt tones. Fire result. Note: In this technique a third layer, a matt of bistre brown ground with isopropyl alcohol, is often used.

**TWO METHODS FOR ETCHING ON FLASHED GLASS**

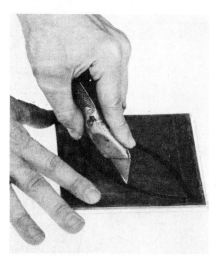

**Con-tact paper. 1a.** Cutting away paper mask with mat knife from areas where etch is desired. Paper covers sides and back to protect against acid.

**2a.** Etching the glass in acid bath. Remove with rubber gloves or tongs. Check gloves periodically by filling with water to make certain no holes exist.

**3a.** Etched piece with residue on left half partially removed, and prior to removal of remaining paper. After removing paper, thoroughly rinse off acid.

**Asphaltum varnish. 1b.** Asphaltum is brushed or dripped onto areas that are to be protected from acid, thus giving choice of controlled or free design.

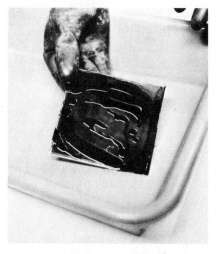

**2b.** Etching glass in acid bath. Areas unprotected by the asphaltum will be etched. Asphaltum can be diluted before application for varied effects.

**3b.** Etched piece with residue on right half partially removed. Asphaltum is removed with paint thinner, rags, and newspaper.

Because isopropyl evaporates so rapidly, it leaves the paint sitting very lightly on the surface. It can be removed where desired with fine-haired brushes that do not disturb the gum layers beneath. The third matt provides strong dark areas. Fire the result.

## ETCHING

Etching is a process that utilizes hydrofluoric acid for a controlled erosion of glass surface. Flashed glass, which consists of more than one layer of glass, is used principally. By etching the thin flash layer, more than one color is revealed.

The acid must be used *with caution.* When not in use, keep in a covered plastic container. Work in a well-ventilated area. Wear rubber gloves, a rubber apron, and if you wear eyeglasses with glass lenses, consider plastic goggles. Don't inhale fumes. Should acid spill on you, flush with water immediately (keep handy in pail) and apply a neutralizing paste of baking soda mixed with water. Though the acid is reused until it is too weak to etch satisfactorily, it is a good idea to add baking soda before disposal to neutralize it.

All areas that are not to be etched must be covered to protect them from the acid. Resists such as Con-tact paper or asphaltum varnish, a black tarlike substance, can be used (see photos, facing page). Wrap transparent Con-tact paper around the glass, pressing it so that it adheres smoothly. Place wrapped glass over cartoon and cut paper away from areas to be etched. When using asphaltum, brush or drip it on the glass, leaving exposed those areas to be etched. Allow asphaltum to dry. Cover back and sides of glass with Con-tact paper to seal against acid, paying particular attention to edges and corners.

Prepare the acid and water solution in a plastic tray in an amount sufficient to cover the piece completely. *Always add acid to water.* Stir slowly with plastic tongs or a wooden stick. Strength of solution depends on the thickness of flash, the quality of line you hope to achieve, and the speed at which you want to cut. Acid can also be purchased in solutions of varying strength.

Immerse the piece, design side up, being careful not to splash solution, and cover. Etching proceeds quickly. Gas bubbles soon form on the exposed glass, indicating that acid is eating through. Brush them off occasionally with a feather or soft brush as they retard etch. The piece can also be immersed design side down; if so, elevate it on small sections of lead came to allow the glass being etched to fall off. However, you will probably want to observe the etching process and will therefore want to work face up. The length of time in solution depends on the strength of the acid and the depth of etch desired.

At completion of etch, take glass from bath with tongs or gloved hands and submerge it in the pail of water. This water should be changed frequently. When glass is cleaned of acid, peel off Con-tact paper, or remove asphaltum with paint thinner, rags, and newspaper.

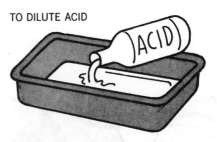

TO DILUTE ACID

*Always* add acid to water, *never* reverse.

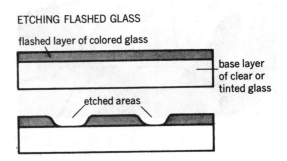

ETCHING FLASHED GLASS
flashed layer of colored glass
base layer of clear or tinted glass
etched areas

Detail. Window by Marco Zubar. Colors and color gradation achieved solely by etching and sandblasting.

Leaded panel by Erik Erikson. Viewed above in natural light. There is some loss of visible glass texture and a color sameness when seen below in artificial light.

# Design

This section provides a framework for organizing visual elements in a manner that is appropriate to the nature of stained glass, its character, and its construction. Its main purpose is to help you understand the design considerations involved so that you can have the gratification of executing your own ideas.

### DESIGN CONSIDERATIONS

Designing is sometimes spoken of as intuitive. What is usually meant by this is that designing is done with the emotions or feelings and without thought. This viewpoint is incorrect, because everything we do involves thought. Some things we "know" from personal experience, others from outside authority, and still others we guess at. When a thought process happens so fast that we cannot separate the elements, we call it intuition. Theory and practice, however, are always involved.

To design is to conceive and plan out in the mind. Design—the arranging and combining of various elements to produce a result—includes consideration of what the finished piece will look like, how it will be put together, and how it will be used. For example, stained glass as a window will admit light as well as keep out wind, rain, and cold. The choice of dark- or light-colored glass will often depend on how much interior light is wanted without having to resort to artificial light. Stained glass as a lampshade provides decorative accents, but also shields the eye from a light bulb's glare and directs the light rays.

As previously stated, how something looks is determined in part by how it is put together. For example, a stained glass window is assembled in sections and each section is assembled of pieces. This procedure becomes a determinant of its design. The result, in the case of the medieval medallion window, was the geometric breakup of the window area into regular, modular, and repetitive units (see photo, page 5). In other words, when designing, once you have the overall shape, you can subdivide the area into separate units and the units into different shapes and colors. The individual units are then put together and assembled into a whole.

Some common design considerations follow; the photos referred to are on page 33.

**Area shape.** The shape of the area will dictate the basic design, whether in relationship to an architectural space or within another given area. At top left, a simple subdivision of color areas works in harmony with a rectangular-shaped architectural opening.

**Combining basic shapes.** One way to combine basic shapes is seen in the window at top right, page 33. Here circles and axial diagonals are combined individually within square modules. The basic shapes,

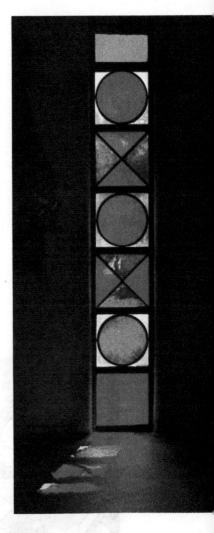

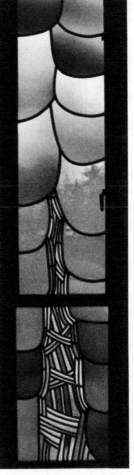

Two leaded windows. (Top left) Note relationship of glass shapes to shape of window area. (Top right) Repetition of shapes with color variations. By Erik Erikson for Jack Lenor Larsen house.

(Far left) Panel for window. Horizontally and vertically arranged glass strips create circular forms. 32″ × 72″. By Richard Avidon. (Left) Two motifs in unified design. Color derived essentially from exterior rather than from glass. By Sam Wiener.

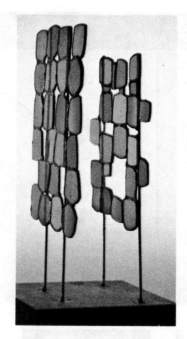

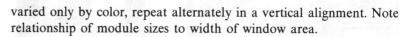
Glass sculpture. Transparent glass mounted in two planes. About 18″ × 8″ from base to top. By Marlene Hoffman.

varied only by color, repeat alternately in a vertical alignment. Note relationship of module sizes to width of window area.

**One shape creating two.** This example (bottom left, page 33) is an intricate arrangement of straight glass strips cut at certain points to form large circles within straight lines.

**Combining motifs.** In the window at bottom right, page 33, large curved shapes are contrasted with small grouped pieces. The two areas relate well to each other even though the design elements are dissimilar.

## COLOR AND LIGHT

The single most important visual element in a stained glass piece is color; the form is a vehicle for color. Understanding color involves understanding light. In contrast to a painting, which reflects light, a stained glass window, by virtue of being between the viewer and the source of light, becomes the light. Interaction of colors is as dependent on the quality of light as it is on the nature of the particular colors combined, the size of each color area, the brightness of respective colors, the distance of the viewer, and the number of colors used.

Natural light is the most exciting light source for stained glass. It causes abrupt changes in color as it streams through the glass, expanding, spreading, radiating. Each color has its own character; dramatic variations, including visual mixtures, are created as the changing light emphasizes some colors while causing others to recede.

"Gateless Gate." Leaded panel with three variations of one motif, with lavish mixture of color. By Carol Caroling. Collection, Alfred Keith.

Probably the quickest way to develop a sense of color is to repeat simple design combinations many times, with variations, and to gradually increase the complexity of color relationships. A variety of preliminary sketches can also be worked out in watercolors or with colored paper pasted on a board. These sketches will serve to simulate in part the final result, as well as to act as guides for determining design. They cannot, of course, be used to determine accurately the final color because they cannot achieve the effect of stained glass.

## SKETCH AND LAYOUT

The sketch is a rendering in color and/or line, drawn to a convenient scale and to the correct proportions so that it can be easily scaled up to a full-size layout. For example, if it is your plan to make a 4' × 2½' window panel, you could choose a scale of 1″ = 1′, which means that every inch of the sketch would be equal to every foot of the panel. The proportionate size of the sketch would then be 4″ × 2½″. If this is too small, then increase the scale to 1½″ or 2″ = 1′. A 12″ rule can be used to figure scale, but an architectural scale rule is much easier to use. It presents ten different scales, as well as inches.

To enlarge the sketch to a full-size layout, divide it into equal parts by drawing over it a grid, or series of squares. Draw the same number of grids, but in proportionately larger squares, on cartoon paper, then reproduce the design, square by square.

## GLASS EASEL

While it is possible to select colors simply by looking at your design sketch and then cutting and otherwise preparing the glass without checking it against different light sources, a more organized approach is desirable. Such an approach involves the use of a glass easel—a sheet of clear plate glass upon which the colored glass is adhered for selecting, viewing, and painting purposes. A 2' × 2' sheet of ¼″ plate glass makes a good-sized easel for small projects.

For selecting purposes, place tiny balls of plasticene at the corners of the colored glass and adhere the glass to the easel. Or use caulking compound (Concord CP 56.6 sealant type). Test colors against natural and artificial light by placing easel against a window and then flat on a light box. If you are just testing colors over a light box, then the adhesive is not necessary.

For viewing the glass, tape reverse tracing (pages 38–39) to easel. Turn easel over and, with black tempera paint and a brush, indicate the lines and borders of the design (for a leaded piece use a brush that approximates thickness of lead lines). You will be painting a reverse design since it will be worked on from the opposite side. When paint has dried, set easel against light source. Then, as each piece of glass is cut, adhere it to easel in proper design area. In this way you can examine piece against piece as you work along, view the entire composition in glass, and make any desired changes.

Leaded window panel with textured, colorless glass. Designed to achieve curvilinear motif, in contrast to rectangular frame. By Harriet Hyams.

## DESIGN EXERCISES

The exercises below are examples of axial and modular, or unit, design. Suggested beginning size is 3″ square. Shading indicates color.

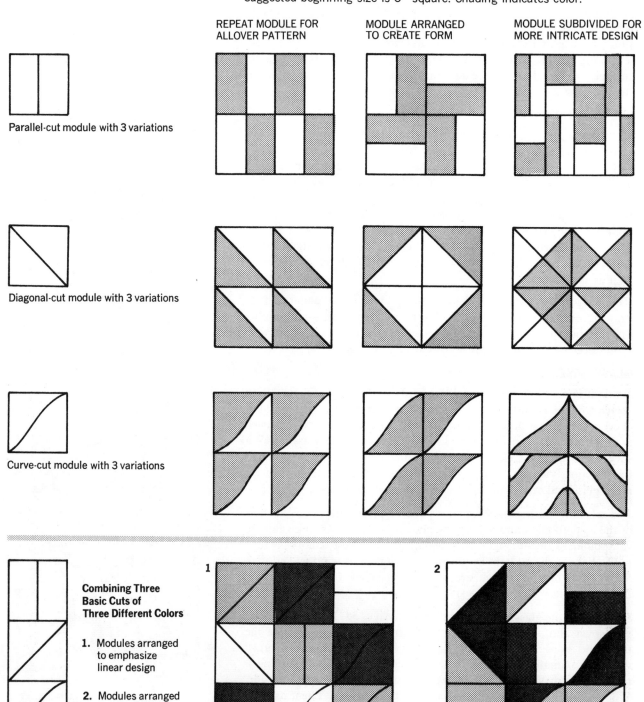

REPEAT MODULE FOR
ALLOVER PATTERN

MODULE ARRANGED
TO CREATE FORM

MODULE SUBDIVIDED FOR
MORE INTRICATE DESIGN

Parallel-cut module with 3 variations

Diagonal-cut module with 3 variations

Curve-cut module with 3 variations

**Combining Three Basic Cuts of Three Different Colors**

1. Modules arranged to emphasize linear design

2. Modules arranged to emphasize color design

When completed design has been inspected, revised, and approved, lay easel flat and remove adhesive. The piece is then ready to be assembled. For use of easel in painting technique, see page 27.

## DESIGN EXERCISES

The exercises on the facing page are based on combining modules for a stained glass piece. Note that they are geared toward working progressively. The initial simple unit and those that follow can be similarly repeated in a variety of color and modular subdivisions. Several results can subsequently be assembled into a larger, more complex whole. Combinations of units form larger units that may themselves be repeated. The result is often an unexpected surprise.

Units can be any geometric shape. For more complex panels, two or more units can be incorporated within other units for a repeat pattern. The mural below includes rectangular and square units, subdivided by diagonal cuts. It indicates the complexity that can result from using two simple modules and only one cut, as shown in the second example on the facing page.

For the beginner, it is best to concentrate on combining units of one shape; further subdivision can be included later. In this way a logical approach to design is established, and much of the initial confusion eliminated at the outset.

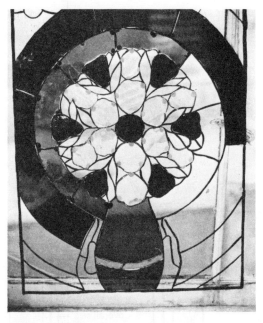

Each piece of glass is mounted on easel, as it is cut, for complete viewing prior to leading.

Clear, colored, and mirror glass used in leaded mural, 10' × 20'. By Erik Erikson for the C. E. Lummus Co., Bloomfield, N.J.

# Cartoons and Patterns

Once the design sketch is completed and the dimensions of your project have been determined, proceed to scale up the sketch (page 35) to full size. The tracing that will be taken from this full-size drawing is called a cartoon, and it will serve as a guide for tracing the pattern and assembly diagrams. The first will be cut up into individual patterns for cutting the glass pieces, and the second is kept as a guide for assembling the glass pieces. Keep the cartoons for future reference or for repetition of design.

**Tools and Materials:** T square, right triangle, masking tape, heavy tracing paper, carbon paper, oak tag and brown wrapping paper, pushpins or ⅝″ carpet tacks, homasote, double-bladed pattern shears, mat knife, tack hammer, straightedge, spring clamp (optional).

## FOR LEAD CAME

### Laying out cartoon

**1.** Align full-size drawing on drawing surface with T square and right triangle. Attach at corners with masking tape.

**2.** Cut a sheet of tracing paper at least 2″ larger around than the drawing. Place over drawing and attach with masking tape.

**3.** Trace along the center of all lead lines, with the exception of those on the outside edges. Along those edges, draw three parallel lines (see diagram). The purpose of the lines is as follows:

Line A (sight size)—indicates the glass that will be visible.
Line B (glass size)—indicates the outer edge of glass that will be hidden beneath lead came flange.
Line C (overall size)—indicates the outside edge of panel.

At this point it is necessary to decide on a specific lead came; ¼″ flat lead came is suggested for the beginner. Measurements would then be those shown in the diagram.

**4.** Lift tracing paper and remove drawing.

**Making the patterns.** The next step is to transfer the cartoon tracing to oak tag paper and brown wrapping paper. The first will become the cutting pattern and the second the assembly diagram.

**1.** Tape oak tag paper onto the drawing surface under the tracing. Cover oak tag with carbon paper (carbon side down), then overlay the carbon with brown wrapping paper. Tape two carbons to the brown wrapping paper, one carbon side down, the other carbon side up. The result should be the paper sandwich shown in diagram, opposite page.

The top carbon will make a reverse design on the tracing paper. This tracing can serve as a guide for painting the design on the reverse side of a glass easel so that the glass pieces can be properly

GUIDE FOR PLANNING CARTOON

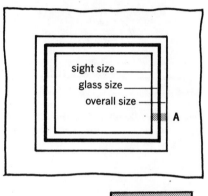

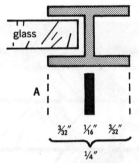

Parallel lines around design perimeter are indicators of sizes. Heart of came measurement is necessary for accurate cutting.

positioned. Note: If instead of oak tag paper, you use Kraft paper taken from a large roll, it will have a curve to it. Be certain to lay it curve side down, as it is difficult to run a glass cutter accurately along an edge that curls up.

2. Trace over all the lead lines and the three outer lines of the design. Number every piece in the design in order to keep track of the patterns. This is especially important when there are many pieces of similar shapes. You may also want to indicate glass colors. Press down fairly hard with pen or pencil so that lines, numbers, and color codes register all the way through to the oak tag paper.

### Cutting patterns for glass

1. Affix assembly diagram to homasote (2′ × 2′ is a good size for small projects). Use pushpins or carpet tacks and tacking hammer.

2. Place pattern paper on cutting surface. With straightedge as a guide, cut along the outside line that indicates the glass size (*not* overall size; *not* sight size; but *glass size*). Use mat knife, X-Acto knife, or single-edge razor blade. To secure straightedge, use a spring clamp at one end and your hand at the other.

3. To cut along the lines that subdivide the numbered areas of the design, use double-bladed pattern shears (see Tools, page 15). You will find it easier to make a continuous cut by cutting near the point where the blades swivel than by cutting with the tip of the blade or attempting to cut along the entire length of the blade.

The pattern shears are unique to leaded glass fabrication; the center blade cuts a section of the pattern equal to the thickness of the heart of lead came. In this way the overall size of the project can be accurately maintained. The shears come in two sizes (sizes refer to the thickness of the center blade that cuts away the strip of paper): the thicker blade allows more play between the glass and the heart of lead came and is used for wide-flanged came only. Use of the narrower blade, however, achieves greater accuracy. As a substitute for the shears, you can make a double-edged cutter by taping two single-edge razor blades together with a ¹⁄₁₆″ piece of cardboard between.

To keep track of the patterns as they are cut, place them on the assembly diagram in their respective numbered positions. Use pushpins or carpet tacks.

### FOR COPPER FOIL (and other flat glass techniques)

The procedure is the same as for lead came, except that the lines of the design are much thinner and more delicate and will not vary in thickness to the extent possible with the lead lines. Two thicknesses of copper foil do not equal the ¹⁄₁₆″ thickness of the heart of the came, so it is not necessary to use the pattern shears. Regular scissors or a mat knife will do. However, some glass artisans prefer pattern shears.

TRACING CARTOON

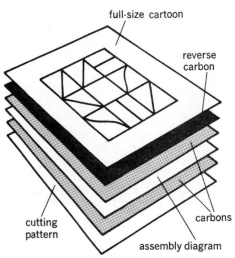

Method of layering a paper sandwich of carbons and paper to make assembly diagram and cutting pattern for glass.

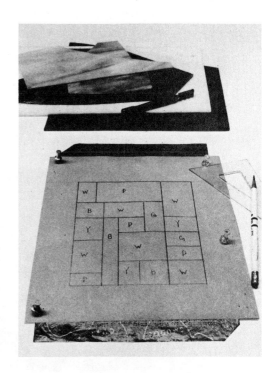

Cartoon can be pinned or taped down for tracing. Note color coding. Number pieces for easy identification.

**Two ways to hold glass cutter: 1.** (Left) Between first two fingers. **2.** (Right) With all four fingers. Hold perpendicular to glass and dip cutter in lubricant between cuts.

# Glass Cutting

Glass cutting consists of scoring the surface of the glass with a glass cutter and then snapping it by applying pressure along the score. Practice first on window glass; it is cheaper.

**Tools and Materials:** glass cutter, glass pliers, grozing pliers, cutting surface, straightedge, bench brush, spring clamp (optional).

**Glass cutter.** Steel wheel cutters (see Tools, page 14) have wooden, metal, or plastic handles. Some metal handles have a ball end that is useful for tapping the underside of the glass to fracture the cut. Diamond cutters are also available, but the steel wheel is more than sufficient. Keep cutter in a small jar with kerosene-soaked cotton so that wheel remains lubricated. *Dip cutter between cuts.* When the cutter dulls, it is more practical to buy a new one. You may, however, try to resharpen wheel by running it up and down an oilstone at a 45° angle, then reversing the angle to sharpen the other side.

**Holding cutter.** There are two ways that cutters are usually held. The first (photo 1) is between first two fingers and thumb. Support hand on last two fingers. The second (photo 2) is by grasping shaft with all four fingers, topping it with thumb. Support hand on small wrist bone. You may find this way affords the most control, at least in the beginning. After a while, you may not need the support. Note: Stand while cutting. *Hold cutter perpendicular to glass.*

**Scoring.** A somewhat pliable cutting surface is desirable. Newspapers or a magazine will do for smaller pieces and homasote or a rug for larger ones. If you have a workbench just for cutting, cover with homasote. *Clean glass thoroughly before scoring.* With pattern held firmly near glass edge, begin score *just inside* that edge. Cutting is done on smoother side of glass.

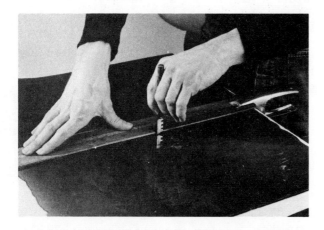

**3. Scoring large sheet.** Note straightedge held down on one end with hand and on other with spring clamp.

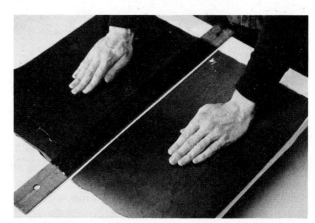

**4. Snapping large sheet.** Guide placed under glass and to left of score, with hands centered on either side.

Usually the cutter is drawn toward you, but push it away if you prefer. Move in a *single continuous motion* from one edge of the glass to the other, rolling past the pattern and off the glass. *Do not start and stop. Do not run cutter over score a second time.* Either will ruin the score and dull the cutter. *Make only one score at a time,* then snap glass before making another. The cutter can be moved quite rapidly, but to do this and follow a pattern requires practice. If cutter is in continuous motion and pressure is sufficient, move as slowly as you like. Degree of pressure varies with different types of glass. You will become sensitive to the proper degree through practice. It is often possible to hear a successful score; the glass "sings."

On certain hard glasses, such as selenium reds or yellows, there is little or no indication of scoring. For these, score glass as usual, then tap the underside with ball end of cutter until a crack forms. If glass will not snap, tap the crack for full length of score line. In flashed glass—a thick layer topped with a thin one—score on thick side. To determine thick layer, move glass edge about in light. Chip a corner if necessary.

**Snapping glass.** Hold glass with score perpendicular to body. Make a fist of each hand, clenched fingers below glass, thumbs over, and place as close to either side of score as possible. Locate thumbs over knuckles of index fingers. Roll wrist outwards, exerting pressure against glass between thumb and index fingers. If score is good, a moderate downward pressure should snap glass cleanly in two. As a precaution against cuts, rasp both edges against each other. Note: The main obstacle when snapping glass by hand is imagining yourself with gashed fingers. If you keep your fingers curled, this is not likely to happen, but do expect a few scratches in the overall process of cutting glass. Use bench brush to clear away glass slivers.

**Large sheets.** To facilitate storage of large sheets of glass and to reduce their size in order to work with them, halve them with straight-line cuts, then halve them again. Using a wooden straightedge as guide, score glass along its complete length (photo 3), then snap in one of two ways: (1) Lift glass, sliding straightedge directly under and to left of score. Center hands on each side of glass, holding it down and keeping fingers close together as a precaution against possible irregular breaking of glass (photo 4). The right side of the glass will be slightly raised. Exert a sudden downward pressure to snap piece in half. (2) Move glass so that score line lies just along workbench edge. Grasp sheet with a wide grip along edge nearest you, raise sheet slightly, and snap with a downward pressure toward edge of bench. Wear gloves as a precaution.

**Glass pliers.** Their most important function is to cut pieces of glass too small to grasp by hand and to break remnants along the cut line. The pliers (see Tools, page 14) have no teeth and meet only at the end where the parallel jaws grip the glass. Extend jaws to score line and, with a combined grip and leverage, snap the glass (photo 5).

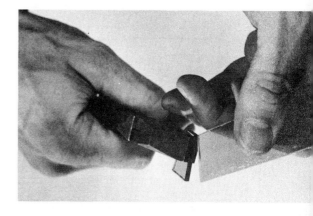

**5. Snapping with glass pliers.** A piece of glass too small to be snapped by hand.

**6. Grozing.** To even an irregular edge. Pliers grind away a little at a time.

**7. Removing sharp edges.** Use carborundum stone or rub edges together.

TO CUT DEEP SHAPES

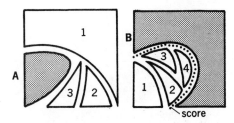

**A.** Make necessary scores to free shape from glass sheet. Cut away according to number.

**B.** Score deep curve. Make inner cuts progressively deeper. Cut away according to number.

**Grozing pliers.** Glass does not always break clean; there tend to be irregularities wherever you tapped or used glass pliers. These must be grozed or they will prevent a good fit of edge to edge when joining. Special grozing pliers are available, but you can also use Utica #620 pliers with the temper removed. Removing the temper softens the metal so that it gradually wears down as it grinds the glass, becoming better to work with the more it is used. Have temper removed by local ironsmith. To groze, hold one handle stationary with thumb and index finger. With remaining fingers on other handle, open pliers and grip glass protrusions. As you close jaws, roll them away from the glass. Jaws move in small chewing movements, grinding away a little glass at a time.

**Curves.** Straight lines or shallow curves are relatively easy to cut, since it is the natural tendency of glass to break along such lines. Both are scored the same way—in one continuous line from one edge of glass to the other. Sharp curves usually need to be tapped. Hold ball end of cutter directly under score and tap gently along its length. As you tap, a "run," or crack, will appear.

An outside curve can be comfortably cut by scoring and tapping as usual (diagram **A**), but when a shape in glass violates the structure of the material, as does a deep inner curve, it is more likely to break. Try tapping the score, but usually a series of lesser curves are necessary (diagram **B**). Tap, then pry out curves with glass pliers, one at a time, from the shallowest to the deepest.

**Circles.** Score circle completely around pattern, then score lines at a tangent to circle. Break pieces off by hand, or tap and use glass pliers. A circle cutter is needed for perfect circles (see Tools, page 14), with the tangent score line done by hand.

**SLAB GLASS**

Slabs are scored in the same way as sheet glass, but breaking requires a chisel-shaped iron wedge set sharp side up into a block of wood or into a large slab made of melted came cutoffs. The edge of the wedge should be perpendicular to your body when breaking slab by hand and parallel to it when using a hammer. Cutting patterns can be traced onto the glass with a grease marker or else held in place by hand or with masking tape. This medium does not lend itself to the same refinement as sheet glass. Exploit its rough-cut quality rather than striving for pristine sharpness. Wear gloves and plastic goggles to protect against flying chips.

**Breaking by hand** (for straight cuts and when glass is sufficiently large). Grasp slab with both hands (photo 1). Bring it down sharply on wedge (photo 2). It should break clean. If not, it was not brought straight down, but at an angle, or not brought down hard enough.

**Breaking with hammer** (for smaller, more irregular pieces). Rest slab on wedge so that score is a fraction of an inch toward your side of wedge. Bring hammer down directly on score. Crucial factors are

Full-sized slab being scored with steel wheel cutter.

**Breaking slab glass. 1.** (Above) Hold so that edge of wedge is directly below score. **2.** (Above right) Raise slab a few inches, then bring down forcefully against wedge.

the angle of the glass to the wedge and the placement and force of hammer blow. To shape glass, see photo 3.

**Faceting.** Slab glass is not always faceted; it is quite handsome as is. But faceting, or chipping the edges, increases the refraction properties and sparkle of the glass. Once the slab has been cut to its predetermined shape, hold on edge on block (photo 4). Strike it ¼″ in or less from glass edge with faceting hammer. When done correctly, a chip will break off, resulting in a curved, striated facet (photo 5). Faceting is usually done only on the face side of the glass; doing both sides presents casting problems. How much to facet is up to you. You could facet all around the piece, or make one or two facets, or just facet an occasional piece.

**3. Shaping.** Hammer on face side over lead block. Pattern on glass as guide.

**4. Faceting.** Strike with hammer on glass edge, not face. Note line that indicates ¼″ depth of facet.

**5.** Facet thins as it moves out in concentric circles. Save scrap for other uses.

# Lead Came

A leaded glass piece is an assemblage of essentially flat pieces of glass held together by means of H-shaped lead came strips. Before being used, the came is stretched in a lead stretcher and its channels are opened with a lathikin. During the fitting of glass and lead, wherever lead meets lead, it is cut with a lead knife. And wherever a cut occurs, the two pieces of came that meet are joined together with solder. Lead came information is on page 20.

**Tools and materials:** lead stretcher, lathikin, lead and stopping knives, plywood, lathing strips, block of wood, small hammer, glazing nails.

**Lead stretcher.** Lead came is stretched to straighten and stiffen it. Stretchers for this purpose are commercially available or may be devised with vise grips or with pliers and nails (see facing page).

**Lead knife.** For cutting lead came. Blades come in different shapes. A semicircular blade is suggested for straight cutting, as pressure can be exerted straight down over the came with a rocking motion, and a hook-shaped blade for intricate cutting while fitting. Some knife handles are lead-weighted on the end. This end is used to tap the glass into the channel, but usually the weighting on a purchased knife is not sufficient, and more lead may have to be melted on.

**Lathikin.** Opens the lead channels so that glass can be fitted. Metal lathikins are available or shape your own out of wood. The homemade one (facing page, top) is sanded and oiled and fits well in the hand.

**Stopping knife.** Pries up the came flanges so that the pieces of glass can be inserted or removed. Also used for puttying and to press down the flanges of flat came after fitting and puttying.

**Tray.** Prior to being leaded, the glass pieces are positioned on assembly diagram in a tray (⅛″ masonite or ¼″ plywood for the base and 1″ × 1″ wood stripping for lip). To accommodate more than one tray under the workbench, channels may be made with L angles, and the trays slipped into them like a series of drawers.

**PANEL.** A panel developed from the design exercise, page 36, makes an easy introduction to leaded glass. Beginning with this project will allow you to progress much more rapidly than if attempting a difficult piece at the outset. A panel in its working stages is on pages 46 and 47. Select the glass for the panel. Make cartoon and diagram (pages 38–39). Cut the glass and wax up each piece on glass easel for viewing (page 35). Place assembly diagram on tray. When completed design has been viewed, remove glass pieces from easel and position them on diagram in tray. Slip diagram out from under the pieces, which remain in position. See steps 1–5, page 46.

### Leading the glass

**1.** Tape assembly diagram to 2′ × 2′ sheet of ½″ or ¾″ plywood. With 45° triangle or roofing square, align diagram about 3″ away

"Angels of the Nativity," contemporary interpretation of traditional lead came window. Artists, Rowan and Irene LeCompte. Craftsman, Melvin Greenland. Installation, National Cathedral, Washington.

from both sides of lower left corner. Align and nail two lathing strips at right angles to diagram along the lower left lines indicating overall size. (Drive nails only partway into plywood to make removal easier. Or double-headed nails may be used.)

**2.** Lock one end of 6′ length of flat came in lead stretcher. Grip with side-cutting pliers at other end; pull to stretch. Open channels by pushing lathikin from end in stretcher toward other end.

**3.** Cut two lengths of the stretched came, measured slightly longer than the sides of the design. These will form the bottom and left sides of the panel. Hold sharp lead knife on came and rock it gently back and forth for a clean slice. Sometimes cutting tends to press flanges down. If this happens, pry them up with needle-nose pliers.

**4.** Place the cut came against lathing strips. At the end of each came length, hammer a glazing nail to hold it in place. Where came meets came in corner, join in either a lap or butt joint (page 20).

**5.** Fit first piece of glass into right angle formed by border lengths. Tap lightly into place with weighted end of lead knife. If glass does not fit readily, use a stopping knife (or thin, bent putty knife) to pry up flanges, and lever glass into place. Position small block of wood against glass and tap with glazing hammer to help obtain a tight fit (wood block prevents chipping of glass).

**6.** Once glass is fitted, cut additional lengths of came for remaining exposed edges. A decision must be made as to which length will extend to accommodate the next piece and which will be cut off. Cut lengths slightly shorter than glass (on one end only) to allow room for next lead, which extends beyond. With this and every succeeding piece, pay attention to the guidelines of assembly diagram. If glass piece extends beyond these lines, consider grozing and sliver cutting, particularly if several panels are to be combined in a large composition where line continuation and overall size is important.

### TOOLS FOR LEAD CAME

1. Lead came strips
2. Lead knife (handmade)
3. Lead knife (commercial)
4. Needle-nose pliers
5. Screwdriver (optional)
6. Stopping knife
7. Glazing hammer
8. Glazing nails
9. Lathikin (handmade)

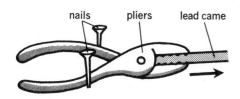

**Stretching lead came.** (Right) Lead in commercial stretcher being pulled with pliers to stretch. (Note lead knife.) (Above) Alternate setup with pliers and nails.

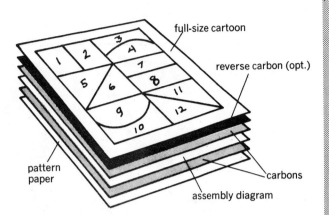

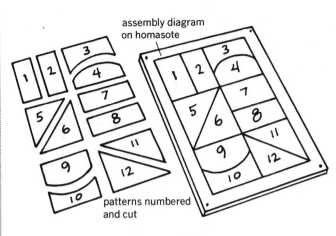

**1. Make carbons.** Trace cartoon for assembly diagram, cutting pattern.

**2. Cut patterns.** Use pattern shears. Mount assembly diagram on homasote.

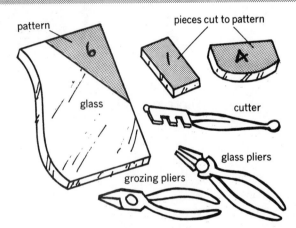

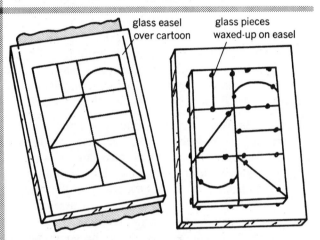

**3. Cut glass.** Place patterns on glass and cut to size. Check against diagram.

**4. Wax up.** Tape reverse carbon to easel. Wax up pieces for viewing.

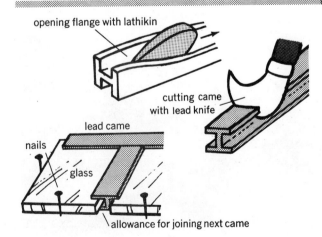

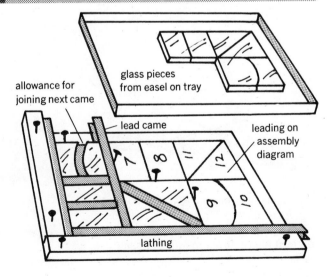

**5. Assemble.** Open channels. Cut lengths. Place glass on tray. Fit glass and lead prior to soldering.

Continue to alternately fit glass and lead by building up from the first piece so that second piece is in relation to first, third in relation to second, and so on. The total structure of the panel is also taken into consideration when fitting successive leads.

**7.** Exercise care as you tap each piece of glass into place with block of wood and hammer or weighted end of lead knife, for as one side is tapped in, the other often slides out. To minimize this possibility and to help keep to lines of diagram, hold lead and glass in place with glazing nails, then renail to hold first the came and then the new piece of glass. Horseshoe nails can be used in place of glazing nails; they are flat-sided and fit very well against glass and lead. Small blocks of wood, the thickness of the glass, are often fitted into the lead channel and the nail driven against the block so as not to mar the came.

**8.** When all the pieces are in place, fit last two came lengths (top and right side) to conform to overall size. Trim excess, then firm panel with two more lathing strips. The piece is now ready for soldering (page 25). Solder on copper wire loops (page 76) if you intend to hang the panel rather than fit it into a frame.

**Puttying and cleaning.** These are best done right after soldering both sides of panel—because all flux residue from soldering should be cleaned off immediately, and waiting would necessitate duplicating the cleaning process, as putty also messes surface. Puttying strengthens the panel, makes it rattle-free, and fills any slight spaces between glass and lead. It is particularly important for windows, as it weatherproofs them and cushions the glass against wind pressure; it is not so necessary for small hanging pieces. A linseed oil putty is recommended, but other caulking compounds are available. Lampblack is used to darken the off-white putty.

**1.** Lay panel on top of newspapers on workbench (preferably not leading bench). Pick up a gob of putty, maneuver a portion of it up to your thumb and force it under the flange. With flat came it is desirable to lift flange with stopping knife. Continue forcing putty into spaces between glass and lead for entire side. Then press flanges tightly down against glass with the stopping knife.

**2.** Remove excess putty along leads with ½″ or ⅜″ wood dowel sharpened to a point in a pencil sharpener. Draw finger behind point to gather up putty. (With half-round came, dowel may pull putty out from under flange. If this happens, draw putty knife along lead instead, forcing putty under at the same time you remove excess.) Turn panel over and putty other side. This will push some putty out the first side and excess will again have to be removed. Putty remains soft, so it will continue to ooze for a while. Keep glass wiped clean with a rag as the oozing oil forms a crust that is difficult to remove when dry.

**3.** After both sides have been puttied, the panel should be cleaned. Dust with whiting (calcium carbonate) to absorb oil from putty and

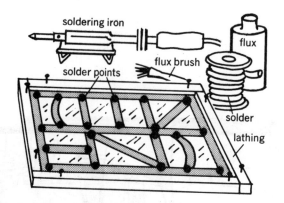

**6. Solder.** Solder all joints front and back. Flux before applying solder.

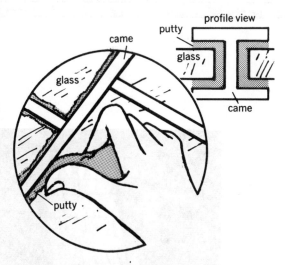

**7. Putty.** Force putty into channels on both sides of panel. Remove excess.

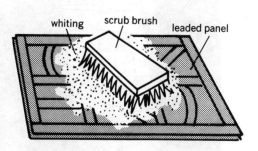

**8. Clean.** Remove flux residue and oil from putty. Panel completed.

any soldering flux residue. With rags and scrub brush, wipe the glass and brush all residue from the lead. Apply more whiting if necessary. (Burlap is a good first rag, sheeting a second.) Turn panel over and clean other side. The use of whiting is not recommended until both sides have been puttied because the fine dust can get

(Above) Abstract leaded panel incorporating a variety of glass sizes and colors, mainly transparent antique glass. By Erik Erikson. 6′ × 1½′.

(Below) Three in a series of leaded windows depicting holiday symbols. By Efrem Weitzman. Each approx. 10″ high. Installation, The Bellerose Jewish Community Center, Floral Park, N.Y.

into the channels of the puttied side and inhibit adhesion of putty to glass and lead.

**4.** Remove excess whiting with a vacuum cleaner. Clean your hands with linseed oil and rags. The oil removes putty and softens hands. Hand cleanser will remove oil. Although wiping with clean rags and then brushing are often enough to clean the glass, an ammonia and water solution may be used for further cleaning and polishing.

**Patina.** Darkening the leads with a patina is really unnecessary; in time they darken by themselves. By day, the light coming through the glass silhouettes the leads. By night, if light is shining on them, they will be more readily seen as a design filigree if they remain lighter than the glass surface. Nevertheless, if you still desire darker leads, you can use antimony trichloride (called "butter of antimony"). It is not readily available, however.

**Turning large panels.** A large panel cannot be simply lifted up and flipped over, especially when only one side has been soldered. Any attempt to do this will cause the panel to sag and the glass will be likely to crack. The correct way to turn a panel is to slide it over the workbench edge until it begins to tip of its own weight. Then, with the edge serving as a fulcrum, quickly tip the panel down to a vertical position. It can then be turned around, its edge extending *up* the side of the bench, and then tipped over flat with the same fulcrum action and slid back onto the bench.

**Large panels.** If you look at leaded glass in old buildings, you will notice that there are panels that have sagged or buckled because lead weakens and stretches with age and continued wind pressure. In order to minimize this possibility, the following general observations are made:

**1.** Short and medium lead lengths that crisscross in opposing directions tend to be more structurally solid than long lengths that continue from edge to edge.

**2.** If long lengths are used, continuous vertical cames are structurally stronger than continuous horizontal cames.

**3.** Interlocking perpendicular leading provides more support than lead converging in acute angles.

**Supports.** Zinc bars are sometimes soldered to a large panel at horizontal intervals from border lead to border lead, or extended beyond to connect with supporting frame. Wind bars, also called stay bars, could be used instead; these are attached during installation. Wind bars are metal braces that are fitted into the architectural opening and are fastened to the panel with copper wire. The wire is soldered onto the panel at particular points before installation.

The maximum suggested size of a panel to be installed without additional reinforcement is approximately 18″ high by 26″ wide. This is also a good maximum size for efficient handling.

Window by Robert Pinart. 5′ × 6′. An example of the virtuosity possible with came. Private house, Reston, Va.

(Detail) Leaded window by David Wilson. Installation, St. Gabriel's Monastery, Brighton, Mass.

Leaded floral window hanging with painted detailing. A simple lead came project.

Lead came lampshade. Translucent and opalescent glass. By S. E. Sayles.

## Floral Window Hanging

Making a small window hanging, or a number of them for a grouping, is a modest project employing both the lead came and painting techniques. Painting is optional, but you might want to take this opportunity to investigate the technique. The graph (opposite) is marked off in inches. Enlarge to suit the size you wish; suggested scale is 1″=3″. Refer to photograph for colors, or choose your own.

Make cartoon, assembly diagram, and cutting pattern; number and color code them. Cut out patterns, then cut glass. If you are painting the flower, see painting technique, pages 26–31. Prepare the lead came and place glass on assembly diagram. Because the flower does not conform to a rectangle, lathing is not used when fitting glass and lead. A plywood form, cut to shape, could be used instead, or just work from the center outward, with nails for firming. Solder all joints, then clean piece. Make a copper loop (page 76) and solder to tip of top petal; string wire through. Hang with small nail or bracket.

## Lead Came Lampshade

A lead came lampshade is fitted flat and is then bent into shape. This type of construction can use large pieces of glass to form the design, while a copper foil shade uses small pieces. In the ten-sided shade shown, each side has five sections: A and C use translucent glass, the rest opalescent. C and E are identical; one inverts for joining. Make a full size layout, then cut out one set of patterns, or templates (right). Cut the glass and lay pieces side by side, forming an almost complete circle, and decide on color order.

Cut horizontal leads to length of circumference. Nail one against lathing and into it fit glass pieces and vertical leads for band D. Omit final lead on end piece of glass. Top band with another horizontal lead. Check dimensions, then tack solder face side. Carefully bend band until unleaded side fits into flange of first piece. Set band upright. Fit band E into bottom flange. Tack solder as you go for this band and succeeding bands. Band E will fold in on itself because of the way the glass was cut. Top other side with U came for a finished look.

Next fit C to other side of D. Top with ⅜″ came to compensate for sharp corners. Fit panel B as others, or make separately (see diagram). Top with U came. Solder a second U came to meet back to back with last one. Fit band A and top with U came. For a finished look flatten a U came and wrap it around the double U came seam. Make any adjustments. Solder all joints front and back. Solder the crossbar for the electrical components to bottom flange of band A and at a vertical seam.

**Floral window hanging.** Scale to size desired. Heavy
lines indicate individual pieces.

LEAD CAME SHADE ASSEMBLY

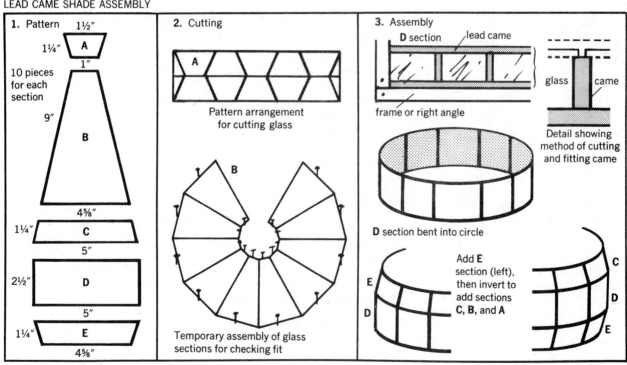

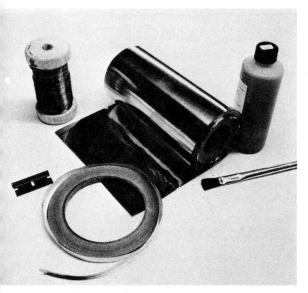

Copper foil comes in rolls 6″ and 12″ wide and in adhesive-backed rolls, 36 yds. long and ³⁄₁₆″, ¼″, or ³⁄₈″ wide.

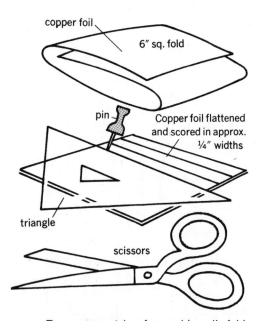

To prepare strips from wide roll, fold foil over three or four times, score widths, and cut along score lines.

# *Copper Foil*

Copper foil resembles lead came in its finished, soldered appearance, but because of the relative thinness of the foil and the resultant narrow margins, it is better suited than the came to small pieces of glass. This material also gives a more rigid support than came and is strong enough to support the weight of a large lampshade. Foil information is on page 21.

**PANEL.** Begin in the same way as with lead came—that is, make a design sketch and cartoon, and select the glass. Then trace the assembly diagram and cutting pattern (pages 38–39), but bear in mind that the lines of the design are much thinner and more delicate and do not vary in thickness to the extent they do with lead came. Number and color code each section, then cut out patterns for the glass cutting. Use regular scissors or a mat knife. Pattern shears can also be used.

Cut the glass carefully to the required shapes (pages 40–42). Edges of adjoining pieces should coincide perfectly for a good result. However, a virtue of this technique for the beginner is that spaces resulting from inaccurate cutting can be filled with solder. After the shapes have been cut, position them on the assembly diagram. Check that the sizes match and, if necessary, groze or trim the glass pieces.

**Tools and Materials:** ¼″ copper foil, lathing strips, glazing nails, tacking hammer, patina, soldering equipment.

**1.** Check glass pieces for sharp corners and briskly grind any with a sharpening stone. Your hands and the glass should be clean and dry, for if either is greasy or wet, the adhesive backing of the foil will not adhere.

**2.** Unroll the foil as you wrap each piece of glass. Allow about ¼″ for overlap. As you wrap, peel off the paper protecting the adhesive backing (or cut copper foil strips from large roll—see left). Wrap strip completely around glass edge, keeping edge centered. Overlap where the ends meet. Cut off excess. On those pieces that will form the panel edges, make certain that overlaps are on the inside, facing another piece, as the heat of the soldering iron can expand the foil at that point and lift it slightly off the glass.

Since the foil is slightly wider than the glass edge, there will be overhangs on both sides of the glass. Crimp and fold these over the edges and press flush with glass surfaces to form neat margins on both sides. Then lay the piece flat and burnish the foil with the handle of the glass cutter or a dull knife so that it lies smooth and tight against the glass. If there is a slight differential where the foil overlaps on glass surface, slice off evenly with razor blade.

**3.** Repeat this procedure for each piece of glass, then position foiled pieces to correspond with numbers on assembly diagram. In a panel where right angles and proper alignment are required, the assembly

**Examples of Copper Foil Technique.** (Above) Lampshade by Susan J. Greenbaum. Base, 18″ in diameter. (Left) Panel by Marlene Hoffman. Approx. 40″ high. (Lower left) Room divider by Lynda Wright. Scrap glass with rondels. 54″ × 20″. (Below) Window panel by Joseph Ferguson. Planes of glass are at different levels, separated and supported by wires.

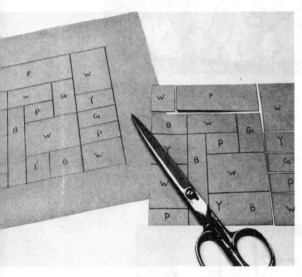

**Make tracings.** Make assembly diagram and cutting patterns. Cut out patterns with regular scissors or mat knife.

**Cut glass.** Cut according to patterns and position on assembly diagram prior to wrapping with copper foil.

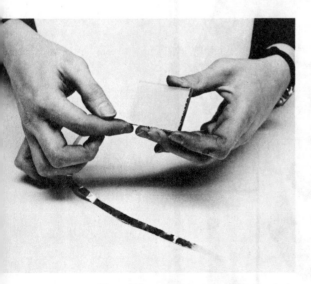

**Wrap glass.** Be sure glass edge is in center of foil strip. Overlap ends and crimp overhangs to surfaces.

**Assemble.** Reposition glass pieces on diagram as they are foiled. Check that dimensions match.

diagram is put down with lathing strips the same as with lead came (pages 44–45) and each foiled piece fitted against another and held in place with glazing nails.

**4.** The panel is now ready to be soldered (page 25). Solder literally floats over all the visible copper and binds the pieces together.

**5.** After the panel has been soldered, it can be edged with U came. Cut the came to size, miter it at the corners, tack solder it to foiled seams, and solder on. Or wrap the edge, as if it were a single piece, with slightly heavier and wider foil or with 18- or 20-gauge copper wire.

If you plan to hang the panel rather than set it into a frame, solder on copper loops at the corners (page 76).

Because of the rigidity and close fit of the solder-coated foil, water-proofing compound is not usually applied. Attempting to apply it will often lift any weak copper edges. It is precisely for this reason that foiled panels are seldom used in exterior walls. When they are, an outside layer of protective storm glass is invariably affixed.

**Patina.** Darken or antique with patina if desired. Patina solution is available at craft suppliers. If you are working in quantity you could make your own—it is cheaper, and you will be able to control its strength. Copper sulfate crystals ground dry and dissolved in water give a copper color; copper nitrate crystals, a dark gray-brown. In most cases, patina is brushed or rubbed with a rag onto the solder. The patina surface can then be polished with lemon oil. Wear rubber gloves, as patina stains the hands.

Finished panel, with three colors of opalescent glass, as window hanging. 8″ square. By Susan J. Greenbaum.

**Solder.** Firm piece with lathing. Float solder over copper surface on both sides. Resolder front for beaded look.

**Patina.** Apply to darken silver color of solder. Panel can be edged with U came, copper wire, or heavier foil.

BASIC SHAPES WITH DESIGN VARIATIONS

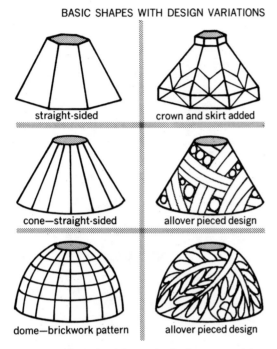

Three basic lampshade shapes: straight-sided, cone, and dome. Shown with variations. Other variations possible.

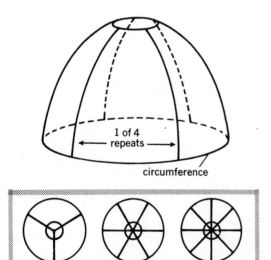

1 of 4 repeats

circumference

3 repeats     6 repeats     8 repeats

**To plan repeat motif.** Divide base circumference to determine size and number of repeats.

## Copper Foil Lampshade

Copper foil is ideal for making lampshades; its flexibility and the resultant ease of wrapping enable many small pieces to be built up around a curved surface. Because glass pieces are cut small, the use of intricate design and color is possible. Forms are used in this technique to determine the shape of the lampshade and to maintain that shape while it is being constructed.

**Design possibilities.** There are three basic shapes for lampshades: straight-sided, cone-shaped, and dome-shaped. They can vary in form and/or in design, as shown to the left.

**1.** *Straight-sided:* lampshades can be square, octagonal, hexagonal, and so on. A crown and skirt can be added.

**2.** *Cone-shaped:* Shades can be made with narrow, straight-sided pieces or with small pieces worked into a pattern around a form. As the shade tapers toward the top, the pieces become smaller.

**3.** *Dome-shaped:* glass pieces can be polygonal and arranged in rows, one above the other. Or they can be free-form and arranged in an allover pieced design. Pieces are made increasingly smaller in size to accommodate the vertical curve of the dome. A band or skirt of a contrasting design can be added. The following basic designs for this shape can also be combined in one lampshade:

*Brickwork design*—glass pieces aligned or staggered like brickwork.
*Allover design*—three or more repeats.

**Forms.** Wooden forms are used professionally but are quite expensive. Styrofoam forms are commercially available and inexpensive. Or an inverted large wooden salad bowl can be used. (A form is not necessary for straight-sided lampshades, but it can be helpful.)

You can also make a plaster form for a dome-shaped lampshade by taking a mold from a glass, plastic, or wooden bowl. A plaster form can be drawn on easily; pins can be stuck into it to hold patterns and pieces of foiled glass in place. It is also less likely to be scorched during soldering and is more sturdy than styrofoam.

To take a plaster mold from the inside of a glass or plastic bowl, mix plaster according to manufacturer's directions and pour it into the bowl (a wooden bowl has to be coated with shellac and vaseline to prevent the plaster from adhering). Allow plaster to set and dry, then invert and use. To take a mold from the outside of the bowl (which is a trifle larger), make a negative mold and then the positive form from the mold.

For a negative mold obtain a cardboard box at least 3″ wider and 2″ deeper than the bowl. Shellac inside of box with two coats. Place inverted bowl in box and tape it down with pressure-sensitive masking tape. A thin coat of vaseline or cake soap may be applied to the cardboard so that it will separate easily from the plaster after casting. Pour enough plaster to cover bowl by at least 1¼″. Let set and dry

## TO CONSTRUCT A STRAIGHT-SIDED LAMPSHADE

**1.** Plan overall lampshade dimensions. **2.** Determine number of sections. **3.** Draw scaled-up cutting pattern. **4.** Cut and assemble glass sections. Foil and solder flat, then fold ends together and solder. (The narrower the sections are, the rounder the shape will be.)

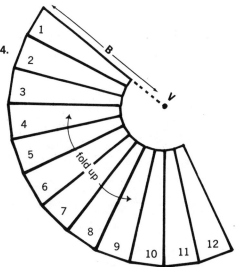

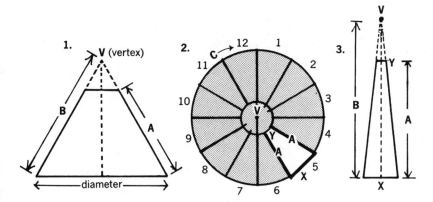

thoroughly. Then remove mold from box; apply two coats of shellac and one of vaseline to the concave part of mold. Pour plaster into concavity to make the positive form. Let dry, invert, and use.

**Template** (full-size guide for making cutting patterns for lampshade). Usually a lampshade consists of three or more repeats. This means that the template need only be ⅓, ¼, or ⅕, etc., of the entire form. It is possible to obtain a commercial template to fit the styrofoam form; its design is printed on paper, and the paper is slit at various places to allow it to conform to the curved surface of the lampshade. Strictly speaking, a flat piece of paper cannot accommodate a sphere, but, with the proper slits, it can approximate it. Remember to leave an opening at the top of the lampshade for electrical components.

Designs for straight-sided lampshades are drawn exactly to size on a flat piece of paper (see diagrams above). In planning a dome-shaped lampshade, however, allowances have to be made in the cutting pattern so that the flat pieces of glass can be fitted onto the curved surface of the form. To plan a brickwork dome-shaped lampshade, decide on the overall size, that is, the diameter and the height. To arrive at the circumference of the base of the lamp, multiply the diameter by the mathematical ratio pi. Pi=3.14. Then determine the number of horizontal rows and vertical sections you want. See diagrams at right for planning and drawing a brickwork cutting pattern for a lampshade.

**Technique** (for allover pieced design; refer to photos on page 58). Working from your design sketch, draw the pattern directly on the form, or cover form first with masking tape (photo 1). Take a tracing from the form of four or five pieces (see top diagram, page 58). Make cutting patterns from the tracing and tack them on the form to check placement (photo 2). Cut the pieces of glass accordingly. Wrap each

## TO PLAN A BRICKWORK LAMPSHADE

**A.** Determine diameter, circumference, no. of horizontal rows, and no. of vertical rows desired. Using protractor, establish base chord width. Angle of chord = 360° divided by no. of vertical rows desired. **B.** Cutting pattern to be scaled-up full size. To allow for dome-shape construction, pattern must be arc-shaped (draw with compass). Note: all bricks are **cut straight.**

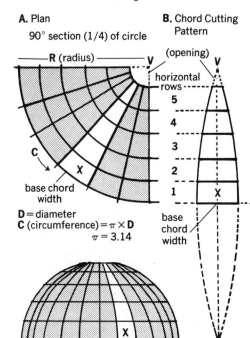

**For allover design. 1.** Four repeats drawn on form wrapped with masking tape.

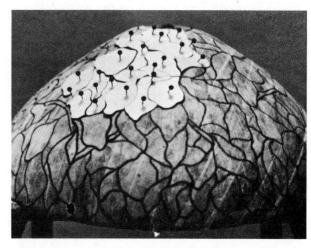

**2.** Cutting patterns tacked onto form for placement and to check fit.

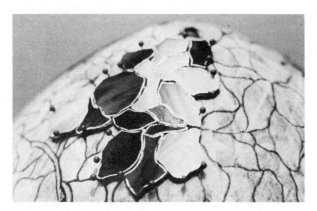

**3.** Cut and foiled glass pieces positioned on form with tacks.

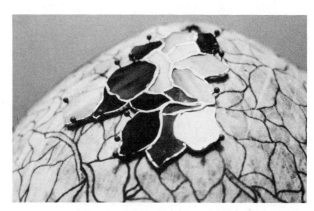

**4.** Glass section tack soldered. Continue section by section until shade is completed.

Tracing for design repeats
and for cutting pattern

tracing

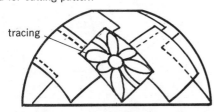

Alternate template
for tracing
design repeats

score line

gesso-coated
aluminum foil

piece with copper foil, position it on the form, and secure it with pushpins or tacks (photo 3). Once the pieces are in place, tack solder them together (page 25). See photo 4.

The next repeat will require a new tracing. Slip tracing paper under the tack-soldered pieces, allowing it to extend to where the next four or five pieces will be attached. Tape paper in place and trace the contour of the completed section, then trace the next four or five pieces that are to be made. Work in a spiral around the form, building a full row around either the bottom or the top. Continue working in this fashion, from the bottom up or from the top down, whichever you find easier, until all pieces are positioned. This method may appear time-consuming, but the advantage is full control over the form, resulting in better fitting of glass pieces.

When all the pieces have been foiled and tack soldered, begin soldering all seams, tipping or turning the form to any convenient angle. When the face side is completely soldered, lift shade off the form and solder the inside. Then, on face side, bead solder. The top and bottom rims of the lampshade can be finished by soldering on copper wire or foil in a slightly heavier gauge.

Clean the lampshade; usually a strong detergent is sufficient. You may have to wash and rinse a couple of times. Patina if desired.

**Alternate template.** If the design is complicated, a sectional template can be made. Smooth some aluminum foil on the form in an amount sufficient to cover repeat section and to extend beyond the area to be traced. Secure with pins. Next cover the foil with muslin, smoothing out all wrinkles first. Apply four coats of gesso and allow to dry thoroughly. Then draw design on gesso-coated form exactly to size. Cut along lines of design (bottom diagram, page 58) with an X-Acto blade or mat knife so that it will lie flat, but do not cut totally apart. Before cutting and flattening template, make certain that dimensions are accurate and that design repeats equally around the form.

Trace design on tracing paper and make as many duplicates as there are repeats. The design can be cut apart and used for patterns. Each piece should be numbered and color coded, and an arrow should be drawn to indicate the grain of the glass if it can be seen.

**Electrical components.** Components and other parts for both hanging and standing lamps are available through stores that sell electrical hardware or that specialize in lamp parts.

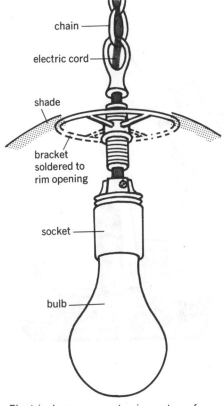

Electrical components in setup for wiring.

Foiled lampshade by Jeff Worob. Three repeats of floral motif with row of brickwork. 24″ diameter, 12″ deep.

Foiled lampshade by Susan J. Green-baum. Unique use of beach pebbles in place of glass. Base diameter 18″.

Copper foil window hangings. "Seagull" and "Tugboat," by S. E. Sayles.

## Three Copper Foil Projects

The following ideas for copper foil flat shape projects are representative of the varied subject possibilities available to the craftsperson in the field of stained glass. The seagull can be used as a window hanging, or a grouping of similar pieces could be made into a mobile. Stained glass jewelry, another possibility, is represented by a belt buckle and a floral pin.

**SEAGULL.** Follow the graph (opposite) and enlarge shape to desired size. Make assembly diagram and cutting pattern, then cut and foil the glass. Use body of bird as the fixed point for positioning foiled pieces. Flux and solder as usual. In order to balance piece, solder on a copper loop (page 76) approximately where shown on graph. String wire through and hang from small nail or bracket. Completed seagull (left) measures 5½″ from wingtip to wingtip and from wingtip to feet.

**BELT BUCKLE.** (Opalescent glass recommended.) Follow usual procedure in making buckle. Since it will be handled a lot, reinforce outer edges with an additional wrapping of slightly heavier foil. To make a slide and hook for the belt, cut lengths from a heavy coat hanger and bend to shape. Use sandpaper to scrape off paint. Position and solder as shown on opposite page.

**FLORAL PIN.** (Opalescent glass recommended.) Follow usual procedure in making pin, then affix a pin back as shown on opposite page. A pendant can be made instead of a pin by soldering on a copper loop (page 76) and stringing a chain or ribbon through.

Examples of jewelry in copper foil technique. (Above) Belt buckle. (Right) Two floral pins of same design but with different colors of glass. By Jeff Worob.

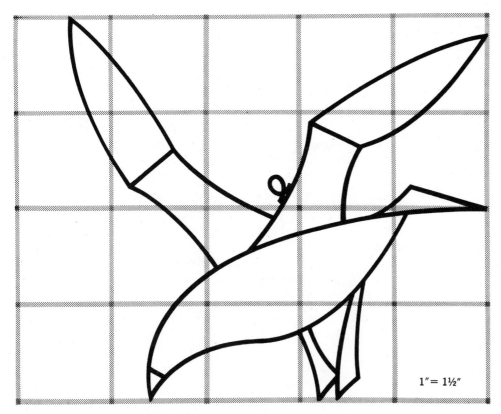

**Seagull.** Scale as desired. Heavy lines indicate individual pieces. Copper wire could be soldered onto wings to mark ribs. Note wire loop for hanging.

1″ = 1½″

BELT BUCKLE ASSEMBLY

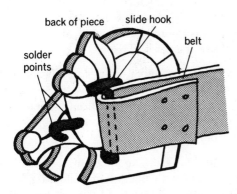

**Belt buckle.** 4″ × 4″. Slide and hook for belt are shaped from heavy metal coat hanger. Paint is sandpapered off. To attach, flux where indicated and position on or across foiled seams. Solder on.

ATTACHING PIN BACK

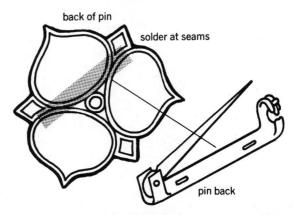

**Floral pin.** A commercially available pin back is soldered to back of piece. Apply flux to center of pin back and position on or across a soldered seam as shown. Or solder on a copper wire loop to make a pendant.

MIRROR / cutaway view

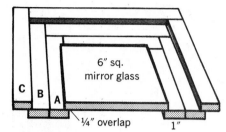

6" sq.
mirror glass

C B A

¼" overlap          1"

**A.** 4 strips—1" x 6¾"
**B.** 4 strips—1" x 8¾"
**C.** 4 strips—1" x 10¾"

**Mirror.** Cutaway view showing method of assembly. Note placement of mirror glass overlapping inner strips, and outer frame overlapping middle strips.

JEWELRY BOX

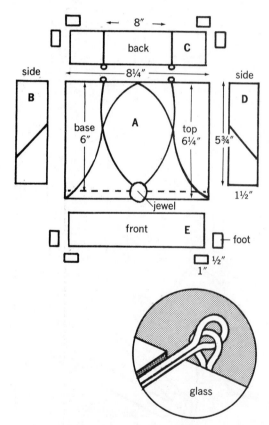

**Jewelry box.** Note that top (A) is cut in seven pieces for design and hinge purposes. Chain is attached to inside seams of A and B (see photo, facing page). Inset shows hinge.

## Mirror Frame

Straight pieces of glass can be combined with mirror glass (which is cut and foiled in the same manner) for the mirror frame project given here.

Cut twelve glass strips to 1" widths and to lengths given in diagram. Wrap strips and mirror glass with copper foil. Remember to check each piece against assembly diagram before and after foiling. Exact fitting is crucial, since strips will butt. Rewrap any piece that does not fit, or groze it, or cut a new one.

Align for soldering with wooden lathing or a right angle metal ruler. The first strips to be positioned and tack soldered together are A and B. Then place mirror glass *on* A, overlapping it by ¼". Next place the C strips on B, overlapping it by ³⁄₁₆". Tack solder both at seams. C can be placed under B for a different result. Solder all seams, front and back. Then patina.

Solder 16-gauge copper wire loops (page 76) to upper back seams. No special backing is necessary for mirror glass, but cardboard or cork can be used to protect coating on mirror back.

## Jewelry Box

This jewelry box is made with straight pieces and simple curves, and presents an opportunity to use marbleized opalescent glass.

Cut the glass to the dimensions given in diagram. Note that side B is cut in two pieces; side C in three. This cutting provides foiled seams for attaching chain and hinges. D is cut to match B. The top of the box (A) is one piece cut into seven pieces in order to include a linear design. It overhangs E slightly so that it can be lifted up easily. A foiled glass jewel is soldered onto seam at overhang. In addition, eight small pieces are cut to form the four feet of the box; each foot is comprised of two pieces. The bottom of the box, cut shorter than the top—since it is minus the overhang—may be made of stained glass, ⅛" clear glass, or mirror glass.

Follow usual procedure in cutting and foiling sides. Then flux and tack solder, first the sides of the box to the bottom and to each other, then each section of each foot to the bottom corners. Always solder onto a seam. Work top separately. Then completely solder all seams of box, inside and out.

To make hinges, cut and tin two 1¾" lengths from 18-gauge copper wire. Grip one length in center with pliers and bend to a U shape. Pinch it about ¼" below loop and twist. Slip other wire through loop and twist for two interlocking twisted wires (see diagram). Pinch loops to narrow them and lessen room for play. Repeat for other hinge. Solder onto box, matching C seams with A seams. Attach chain with solder to inside seams of B and A. Patina all seams, hinges, and chain.

**Completed mirror.** Shown also is a holder for dried flowers comprised of five sides and marble base. (Not waterproof.) Both by S. E. Sayles.

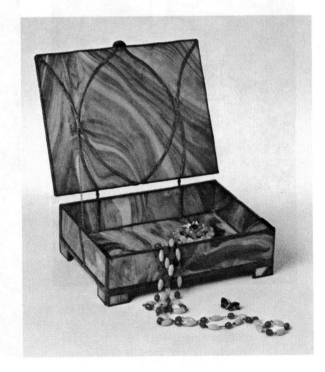

**Completed jewelry box.** Shows use of marbleized opalescent glass. (Right) Box opened. Note hinges and fine chain soldered to side and under top lid. By S. E. Sayles.

(Above) Faceted glass mural for an interior wall, by Sam Wiener.

(Below) Detail of faceted glass door panels, by Erik Erikson. Architect, Jerry Weiss. In epoxy, each 1' × 7'. Geometric tree design adapted from Pennsylvania Dutch motif. For Mahalsky house, Pa.

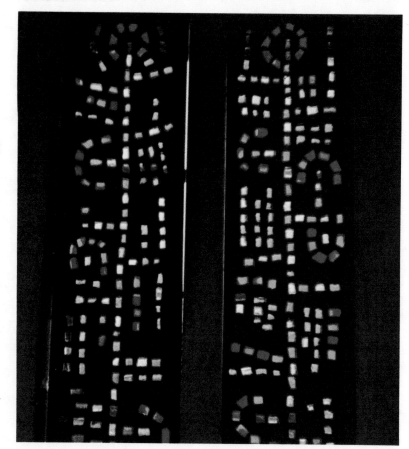

Slab glass window by Efrem Weitzman. One of a series depicting the Covenant of Noah. 1' × 8'. Installation, Temple Israel of the City of New York.

# Slab Glass

Slab glass, also called dalle de verre, chunk glass, or faceted glass, is cast in molds and can be purchased in its cast size, 8″ × 12″ × ¾″, or in remnants. The slab is scored in the same way as sheet glass, but breaking requires a special hammer and a wood block with an upright metal wedge set into it. The cut pieces are then placed within a frame, and liquid plaster, concrete, or epoxy is poured around them.

The fact that a fluid substance is poured around the pieces of slab glass, in contrast to the solid came against which pieces of sheet glass are fitted, is an important design consideration. As the lines of lead came (or copper foil) are lines of design seen against light as black filigree, so the spaces between pieces of slab glass are design shapes seen as black silhouettes as well as thick lines. One asset of this technique is the variety of form possible in the poured spaces as compared to the linear quality of lead and copper lines.

Epoxy or concrete is generally used in an exterior architectural space, whereas plaster is more than substantial for any interior use, such as a room divider composed of several panels.

**PANEL CAST IN PLASTER (using scrap glass).** For a first panel do not concern yourself with cutting the slab to a predetermined design. Instead use scrap glass pieces and arrange them at random on a sheet of ⅛″ plexiglass. Plexiglass is used because plaster will not adhere to it, and, unlike glass, it can be clamped without cracking. It is desirable to keep a first panel small, about 1′ square. The plexiglass should be larger than the panel by at least 1″.

**Tools and Materials:** slab glass scraps, plexiglass, china-marking pencil, wood, Con-tact paper, hammer, plaster.

**1.** With china-marking pencil or other grease marker, indicate panel edge on the plexiglass. Draw another line 1″ in from panel edge. No glass is to be placed beyond this line in order to assure strength around the edges and provide enough space to set panel into a frame.

**2.** Place plexiglass on light box and arrange scraps, allowing at least ¼″ between them for structural strength. Do not rush process. Move pieces about until you arrive at a design you like. Then carefully lift plexiglass (with design in place) onto workbench. Use a carpenter's level to assure that the bench is level for the pouring process.

**3.** With four strips of wood make a frame for the poured matrix (material in which glass is embedded). Frame sides should be at least 1¼″ high. Nail or clamp frame to workbench and over the plexiglass (see diagram). If nailing, use double-headed nails for easy removal. Use bolts if repeated pouring into frame is intended. Square corners with right triangle.

**4.** Apply Con-tact paper to inside edges of frame to prevent adherence of plaster to wood.

"Yucatan," faceted panel, by Mariette Bevington. Note facets on glass edge.

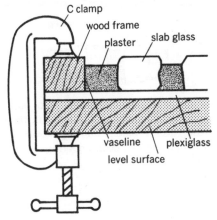

Setup for pouring plaster matrix. Plexiglass is used because plaster will not adhere to it. Be sure surface is level.

**5.** Mix approximately one part plaster to one part water in a plastic container (easiest to clean). Four cupfuls should be enough for a panel 1' square. Plaster should pour easily so as to level off, but not be too runny. The last pour should be the runniest to assure leveling. Pour so that plaster is flush with, but does not cover, slab surfaces. It is not necessary to pour all at once. Take care that pieces are not moved when the plaster is poured around them. Once plaster has set, the frame can be removed, and the panel lifted and viewed.

A distinct advantage to working with plaster is the ease of cleaning the plexiglass, especially while the plaster is still wet. Use sharpened wooden pegs for this. An old toothbrush is also helpful.

**Additional suggestions.** (1) Texture plaster by pouring sand around pieces before pouring plaster. Add more sand to top layer of plaster just as it is setting up. (2) Color plaster with dry powdered tempera, vegetable coloring, or commercial dyes. (3) Carve plaster while wet. (4) To obtain negative sculptural relief, shape plastilene modeling clay and lay shapes on plexiglass. Or cast entire panel on carved plastilene. (5) Embed pebbles, shells, or glass mosaics by laying them down before pouring plaster and/or pushing them into top layer as it is setting up.

**PANEL CAST IN CONCRETE.** The procedure for making a small panel using premixed concrete is the same as for a panel cast in plaster. Follow manufacturer's directions. Liquid silicone is often applied to a completed panel when waterproofing is required.

**PANEL CAST IN EPOXY.** The principal advantage of epoxy is that it bonds to the glass and automatically weatherproofs the panel. The second advantage is weight. A finished panel weighs about one-fifth as much as a comparable concrete panel, making installation understandably less difficult.

The procedure for epoxy is similar to plaster, but there are significant differences. In this instance, work from a predetermined design. Make a cartoon, then an assembly diagram and cutting pattern (pages 38–39). Use a mat knife to cut out patterns. Cut slab glass (pages 42–43). During the casting process, refer to diagrams and photos on this and opposite page. See pages 21–22 for information on epoxy.

**Tools and Materials:** epoxy (resin and hardener), epoxy solvent, wooden framing, fine sand, coarse sand or marble chips, thick tracing paper or tracing cloth, heavy Kraft paper or brown wrapping paper, masking tape, rubber gloves, cardboard, mixing stick, rubber spatula.

**1.** Completely cover workbench with paper (heavy Kraft or brown wrapping) for ease in cleaning up. Lay cartoon down and cover with a sheet of thick tracing paper or tracing cloth to protect it from the epoxy.

**2.** Make a frame with four wood strips, nailing them down along the appropriate edges of cartoon and squaring their corners. Vaseline may

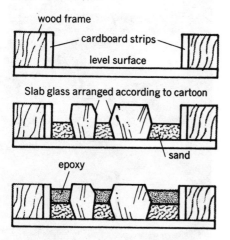

Front side/1st pour

wood frame

cardboard strips

level surface

Slab glass arranged according to cartoon

sand

epoxy

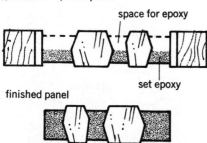

Reverse side / 2nd pour

space for epoxy

set epoxy

finished panel

Setup for pouring epoxy. Two pourings are required; first the front, then the reverse side. Panel is allowed to harden before second pouring.

TO MAKE PAPER FUNNEL

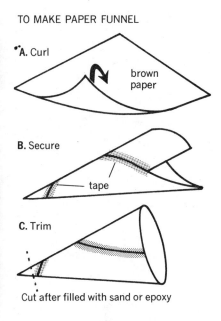

**A.** Curl

brown paper

**B.** Secure

tape

**C.** Trim

Cut after filled with sand or epoxy

**1.** Checking depth of sand layer. Sand is poured through paper funnel and spread to an even thickness of ¼″.

**2.** Directing flow of epoxy onto sanded surface. Flow is controlled by holding fingers at open end of paper funnel.

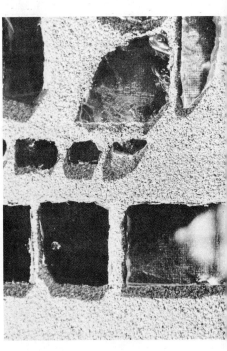

**3.** Texturing panel surface. Sprinkle coarse sand or other granular material onto freshly-poured epoxy.

**4.** Panel turned over for second pouring. Before epoxy is poured, fine sand is brushed away from surface.

**5.** Close-up of completed panel, showing glass in sand-encrusted epoxy. Note that level of epoxy is below glass.

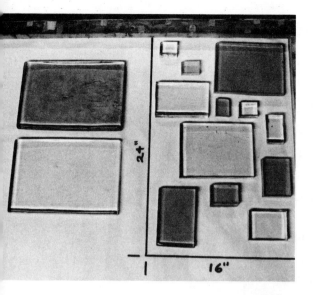

Two slabs cut into successively smaller rectangles and arranged for design.

**Suggested designs.** Use one slab or 2 halves of 2 colors for 16″ square panel.

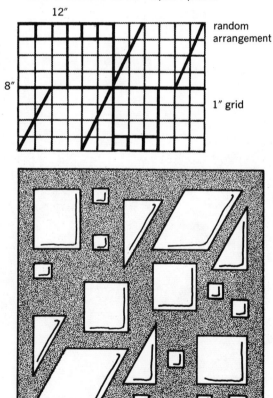

random arrangement

1″ grid

formal arrangement

be applied to inside edges of frame to keep epoxy from adhering, but an alternative is to line frame with thin strips of cardboard. Position glass pieces on cartoon according to design.

**3.** Make a funnel of heavy brown paper and masking tape (see diagram, page 67). Cut funnel tip for a ¼″ to ⅜″ opening. Funnel a ¼″ layer of sand between the pieces of glass. Spread it evenly (photo 1, page 67). The sand should be clean, strained river sand.

The sand keeps the epoxy from adhering to the underlying cartoon and offsets the thermal reaction of the curing epoxy, which could cause cartoon to buckle, resulting in a wrinkled contour on that side of panel. Also, since panel is turned for a second pouring, the sanded surface will facilitate adherence of second layer of epoxy to first. See second diagram, page 66, for depth of sand in relation to glass.

**4.** Make another funnel and use it to direct flow of epoxy between the pieces of slab (photo 2, page 67). As epoxy is quite thick and syrupy, it often has to be helped around the glass with a small piece of cardboard. Pour epoxy to within ⅛″ of glass surface (see third diagram, page 66). Try not to get it on surface, since it is sticky and, therefore, difficult to remove. If needed, use epoxy solvent on a rag, being careful not to move glass. Discard funnel after use.

**5.** Once epoxy has been poured and smoothed out, sprinkle coarse sand or marble chips on epoxy surface until epoxy can no longer be seen (photo 3, page 67). If sand sinks, keep sprinkling until it no longer does so. (This coating textures panel surface. It is not necessary but is generally regarded as more pleasing than plain epoxy surface.)

**6.** Allow panel to harden overnight, then brush away excess coarse sand and save it (photo 4, page 67). Remove frame. Carefully lift panel and turn it over. Brush away excess fine sand and save it. Replace frame and make a new batch of epoxy. Repeat pouring procedure, this time bringing epoxy to within $1/16''$ of glass surface. See fourth diagram, page 66. Coat with coarse sand and allow panel to harden.

## FACETING GLASS

Slab glass is not always faceted (the chipping of glass edges); it is quite handsome without it. But faceting adds another dimension by increasing the refractive properties, and thereby the sparkle, of the glass. Always facet before casting panel. Since the faceted area often falls below the final level of the epoxy, it is sometimes necessary to fill the faceted depressions with plastilene before casting. Remove plastilene when epoxy has hardened. Faceting glass is described on page 43.

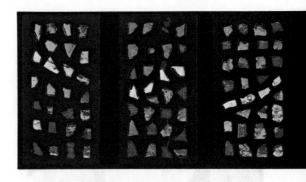

Slab glass pieces, approx. 2″ each, conform to 20″ × 10″ rectangles. Three in a series by Erik Erikson. Note that clear pieces are arranged to visually integrate panels into a total unit.

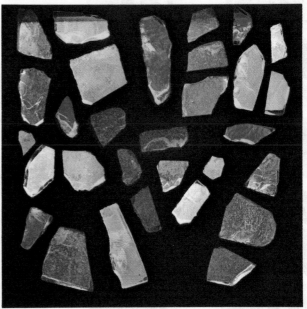

(Left) Faceted concrete screen, 5′ × 7′, artificially lit. Six sections in metal frame, by Mariette Bevington. Installed in apartment house lobby. (Above) Detail of 2′ square section.

(Above) Detail. Mural laminated on one side of plate glass. By Robert Sowers. Installed, Capitol Park South, Washington, D.C. (Left) Two panels laminated on both sides of plate glass, each 1′ × 6′. By David Arnold. Installed, Zimmerman house, Berkeley, Calif. (Below) Detail. Laminated mural by David Arnold, incorporating halved bottles laminated to both sides of plate glass. For Libbey-Owens-Ford Co.

# *Other Techniques*

Of the five techniques that follow, three use crystal clear epoxy for bonding, one a kiln, and another relies on exact fitting of the glass. In some of these techniques, the glass pieces are supported on a sheet of clear plate glass. Make sure all glass used is absolutely clean. When working over a light box, prepare assembly diagram on heavy tracing paper (instead of brown wrapping paper) so that the colors can be seen. For epoxy and firing information, see pages 21–23.

### LAMINATED GLASS

This technique uses epoxy to sandwich flat pieces of colored, textured glass together on a clear glass base. Lamination differs from other flat glass techniques in its use of sharply defined shapes that butt each other without black lines between the pieces. It also offers the opportunity to superimpose colors by laying one glass piece on another.

To improvise a design using scrap glass, begin by selecting a piece of glass and epoxying it immediately onto the clear base. Select another piece and epoxy it somewhere near the first one, or on top of it, or next to it. Work spontaneously, allowing each selection to indicate the next one. Cut the scraps, if you like, to fit against one another. Allow the design to form without effort. Do not forget superimposition—two, three, or four layers, if you want.

However, a good method of designing for this technique is to use colored paper cut into shapes and assembled into collages. Another is to superimpose adhesive-backed color acetate sheets (Bourges or Zipatone) onto clear acetate, working over a light box. Either way will help in the selection of design and colors. Once the design and the different layers are determined in scale, make the full-size drawing, one for each layer. Cut out patterns with a single-edge razor blade to obtain the most accurate meeting of edges possible.

When cutting the glass, try to avoid any need for grozing. Grozing creates an irregular edge that detracts from the possibilities of sharp definition. You can, of course, include an irregular edge in the design, but this should be done intentionally.

Mix specified amount of epoxy. Apply to glass base and press glass piece firmly in place, or apply to glass piece, or to base *and* piece. Use just enough epoxy to bond glass to glass. Too much can result in the excess oozing out from between the pieces and onto the surface; not enough can result in air pockets. Carefully remove any epoxy on the surface with epoxy solvent. Once the piece is placed on the base do not move it. If you are laminating the other side, allow epoxy to harden before turning panel over.

**LAMINATED SCREEN.** The screen shown (right) has a single layer laminated onto either side of the glass base, but more than one layer can be superimposed on either one or both sides. Leave a ¼″ to ½″

DESIGN FOR THREE PANEL SCREEN

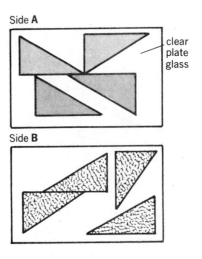

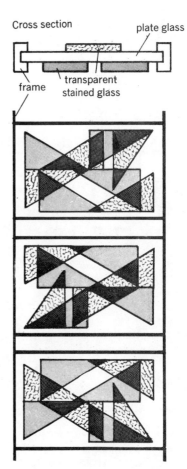

One simple shape, in two or three colors and textures, can made an intricate and exciting design.

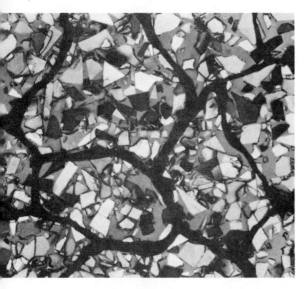

Detail. Panel of scrap glass partially crushed and embedded in clear epoxy, approx. 1″ thick.

Glass mosaic panel with irregular grid pattern. By Mariette Bevington. One of a series. Shown in color, page 13. Commissioned by Abraham & Straus Co.

margin around the edges of the design for fitting the glass into a frame. Make a series of panels for the screen, then fit them into a wooden or metal frame.

## CRUSHED GLASS

Crushed glass is more correctly considered an adjunct to laminated glass than a technique by itself. However, the results are quite different. Whereas lamination results in sharp, distinct edges with visual mixture at the joinings, the laying down of various sized crushed granules causes blending and gradual tonal changes.

Technically, crushed glass is really powder. However, by breaking large glass scraps into successively smaller pieces, a gradual decrease in the size of the glass pieces can be achieved and used as a feature of the final design. As the pieces get smaller and smaller, they more nearly approximate the technical definition of crushed glass.

Crush or break the scraps in a cloth bag with a hammer. Since the pieces are so small, the final effect can be muddied if different colors are crushed together. To avoid this, hammer each color separately and then store in separate containers.

Coat the glass base with epoxy. Place it on the light box over the design. If the glass is in tiny granules, pour it like powder. Small pieces can be stood on edge or laid flat. When all glass is down, pour a coat of clear epoxy to cover completely. The glass should be framed in order to contain the epoxy.

## GLASS MOSAICS

The mosaic technique utilizes small pieces of glass and an opaque epoxy grout, usually with, but sometimes without, a glass base. The linear design created by the grout matrix distinguishes this technique from lamination. Grout comes in different colors, including black.

Scraps can be used as they are, taking advantage of their different shapes, or cut to a predetermined design, either in various shapes or to fit a grid (a framework of rectangles or squares). If you choose the latter, draw a grid on paper to the size mosaics you wish, then place grid under a piece of scrap glass. Score the glass in both directions. Either snap by hand or use glass pliers. Do the same with the other pieces of scrap, keeping each color in a separate container. As you plan the design, you can vary the sizes and colors of the glass or create separate areas, each of a different color. Keep the glass the same approximate thickness throughout or the surface will be uneven.

**SMALL PANEL WITH BASE.** Work over light box and place design tracing under glass base. Coat base with clear epoxy. Also coat each piece of glass as you position it on base. Adhere securely. Allow to set overnight, then fill in spaces with grout. Remove excess grout with a rag dipped in epoxy solvent. Allow grout to set.

**SMALL PANEL WITHOUT BASE.** Place design tracing on light box; tape transparent Con-tact paper (adhesive side up) over it. Arrange glass pieces on adhesive surface in a mosaic fashion, with irregular spaces between them. Fill these spaces with epoxy (PC-7, a pasty, sticky epoxy available in hardware stores, is recommended). Note: If you have difficulty with its consistency, thin with manufacturer's solvent. Spread epoxy slightly beyond design perimeter. When set (about eight hours), it will be rubbery and can be trimmed with a knife. Using a rag soaked in water or denatured alcohol, remove any epoxy that remains on the glass surface. Add fine dark gravel to the surface, if desired. Once epoxy has set, peel off Con-tact paper.

## GLASS ASSEMBLAGE

The assemblage method, developed by Fredrica H. Fields, employs layers of glass sandwiched between two sheets of plate glass. Because only translucent or clear glass of good quality is used, the light that travels through the various layers and the intermingling shapes will transmit the purity of color and sparkle inherent in the glass. The light will be fractured and dispersed, so that the work is alive throughout. It is not wise to work in excess of a 30″ square. A smaller work can start from 4″.

Once the length, width, and depth of the work have been decided, a strong, seasoned, hardwood box frame with reinforced corners can be built, with a strong molding along the inside of the back edge to hold the glass. The walls of the frame may vary from 3″ to 6″ or more in depth, according to needs. Stain the inside of the frame a dark color and lay it face up on light box.

First into the frame is a sheet of ¼″ plate glass; the next layer or layers will be choosen from a wide variety of glass—antique, figured crystal sheets, rods, tubes, rings, marbles, jewels, beads, rondels, dalle chips, and so on. Possibilities are endless, each succeeding layer making a vast change in what lies under it. Glass is cut according to design when needed. Nothing is secured, as the panel may be taken apart many times to explore new ideas. Depending on desired effect, space between layers may or may not be called for. A narrow hardwood frame, of whatever depth the airspace is to be, and which fits the outer frame closely, can be dropped into the work to hold layers apart.

When all is resolved, exact fitting is necessary so that final fixing of the glass will prevent movement when the work is lifted into an upright position. The design is then taken apart and each layer is laid out on surrounding surfaces. All glass is washed in ammonia solution, rinsed several times, and polished dry.

The glass is replaced in the frame with minimal use of epoxy where necessary. The final layer will be another sheet of plate glass, its edges sealed to the frame with black plastic tape to prevent entrance of dust and moisture. For ventilation, the rear of the panel is not sealed. Then a narrow hardwood molding, which fits inside the outer frame, is placed against the plate glass and screwed into position.

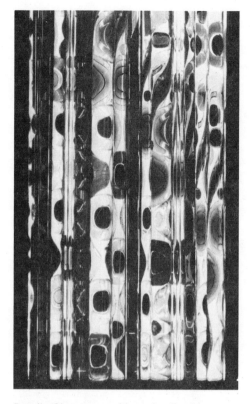

Detail. Glass assemblage by Fredrica H. Fields. Many types of glass layered in box frame, 30″ sq. Top layer clear glass rods. Shown on back cover. Installed, Greenwich Library, Greenwich, Conn.

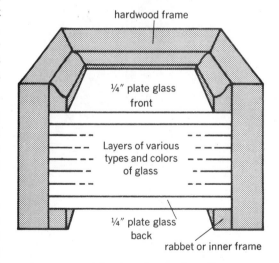

Arrangement for layering and sealing glass assemblage in deep frame.

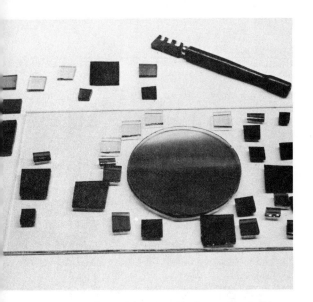

One of four panels for suggested lamp project set up for fusing. The small pieces of glass are fixed on glass base with Duco cement.

Panel with fused colored glass pieces

5″

¼″ brass rod

9″

Completed lamp. Panels joined in copper foil technique with vertical and horizontal supporting brass rods. Bracket for socket soldered to inner base.

## FUSED GLASS

Glass adheres to itself when heated to the proper temperature in a kiln. Fusing literally means to reduce to a liquid state by heat and to blend by melting together. Most important in this technique is the annealing process (gradually cooling glass to remove internal stress); glass too rapidly cooled will crack. Glass should also be heated slowly. Variation in thickness is another consideration. A uniform thickness, resulting from the same number of superimpositions, is less likely to crack than an irregular surface height.

The compatibility of the different glass types also has to be considered. Since each type has its own reaction to heat and rate of expansion, dissimilar types fused together will invariably crack when cooled. If you do not know whether the glass pieces are compatible with each other or not, you will have to experiment. If the work is small, say 3″ square, it is less likely to fracture than a larger panel. Fusing onto a clear glass base will hold the piece together, though cracks often occur where scrap meets base. Another possibility is to pile some pieces in a ceramic container and melt them to become a crazed pool.

**TABLE LAMP** (left). Cut glass scraps according to design and arrange them on ⅛″ window glass. Leave a margin of at least $^3/_{16}$″ to ¼″ around glass to allow for fitting. Repeat for each side of lamp, then fire and anneal. Glass scraps can be used as they are, without being cut, or some can be crushed and sprinkled on the glass where desired. To complete the lamp, the glass panels can be fitted in a soldered frame or they can be held in place with hooks or rings.

**GLASS JEWELS.** Capillary attraction causes glass to rise at a certain temperature, then to melt and flow. If small pieces of glass are arranged separately on a glass base, they will rise into shapes resembling large single drops of water. If the heat continues to rise, these "droplets" will spread out on the surface of the glass base. (If pieces are arranged so that they touch, they will flatten out without forming "droplets.") By using this principle, you can make many small jewels by placing the pieces directly on the kiln shelf (without a glass base) and allowing them to form into "droplets." Be sure to coat shelf with kiln wash to prevent the glass from adhering to it. These jewels can be used as accents in copper foil or lead came projects. They do not require annealing.

**Additional suggestions:** (1) Cut window glass to a series of 1¼″ squares and fuse scrap glass to them. Use as a tabletop or chessboard by epoxying them onto a reflective background and applying grout between. (2) Lay out a design based on a grid of 6″ squares and subsequently assemble the individually fused panels to form a larger panel. (3) Make small pins using a few pieces made without a glass base. Attach pin backs with epoxy.

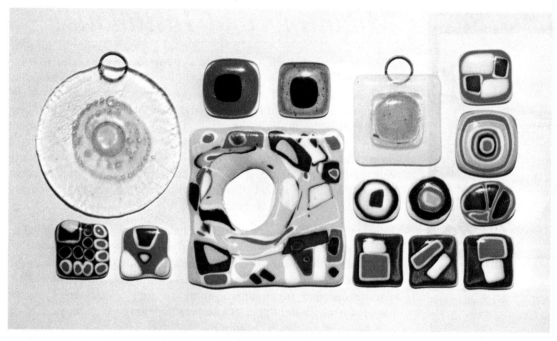

Assortment of melted worked glass by Arthur Tieger. These can be incorporated in panels and in jewelry, such as buckles, pins, or earrings.

(Right) Fused glass panel by Edith Bry. Pieces of glass arranged and layered according to design, fixed with Duco cement, then fired at 1200° F.–1300° F.

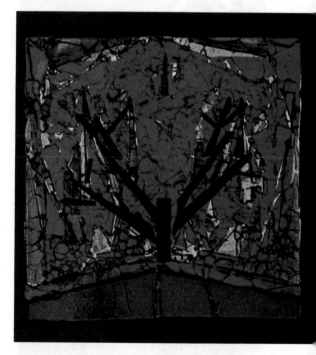

Lampshade by Jack Cushen. Sheet glass slumped (curved by heat on kiln form). Flat glass foiled and soldered in seams where dome cracked during annealing. Here accidental cracking was used to advantage. 14″ × 9″.

Reinforced silhouette panel in removable wooden frame. Installed against existing window. By Erik Erikson.

Faceted glass window panels. From a series, installed in Staten Island Hospital chapel. By Mariette Bevington.

# Mounting and Installation

The simplest installation for a leaded panel is to construct a wooden frame the size of the window opening, install the stained glass panel in it, and then fasten the frame onto the interior sill. It is usually not possible to install a leaded panel directly into an existing window frame, since the mullions are made for ⅛″ window glass and there is not enough room for the thickness of the came. To construct a simple frame, you need only butt and nail four pieces of molding and reinforce the angles with angle irons. Strips of ½″ × ½″ wood, called "stops," are nailed into the frame (see facing page) to contain the panel front and rear.

Existing window frames will usually accommodate a copper-foiled or fused glass panel. For a laminated one, you could remove the window, sash and all, from the window frame and laminate directly onto the glass. A slab glass panel, which obviously could not be accommodated, can be installed in an architectural opening (see diagram, facing page). Installation in an architectural opening is predicated on a number of variables, including the glass technique used, the size and shape of the opening, and the materials—such as stone, metal, or wood—into which the glass is to be installed.

For interior installation you can suspend panels by picture wire from the ceiling, or install them in free-standing metal or wooden frames.

**Copper wire loops.** Panels or free-form objects that are not to be framed can be hung by string, wire, or plastic fishline through copper wire loops. The wire gauge will vary with the weight of the piece. A small piece, for example, might require about a #20 or #21 wire; a large heavy panel, about a #16 wire. The thinner the wire, the higher the gauge number.

To make a loop, clean wire with steel wool and cut a 3″ length. Bend the length in half to form a loop. Twist the wire just below the loop twice around with needle-nose pliers. Tin the loop with solder and attach. For corners, twist wires to form right angles to the loop.

For a small lead came panel, first use a knife to scrape clean the outside channel of the came (if flat came) where you intend to solder the loops. Flux both wire and came. Hold loop with pliers and apply a glob of solder to each end of the wire. Support panel in a vertical position. With soldering iron, join one end of wire to bottom of came channel. Solder to a joint or as close to one as possible. Turn panel onto its side and join second end of wire. Repeat for second loop.

For a copper foil panel, just wipe clean and apply flux. Solder at the seams. For free-form pieces that require only one loop, solder the loop at whatever point will give balance.

# *Care and Repair*

If a window is well made and securely and properly fitted, it does not require much attention. However, weather, settling, and normal stress may in time cause some cracks and buckling to occur. You may also have purchased a section of an old panel that needs repair and that you wish to incorporate into a new piece.

Removing an entire window for releading can mean more broken pieces; therefore, interim measures should be taken. One such measure, not limited to stained glass, is to use what is called a Dutchman—a device for hiding or counteracting structural defects. The Dutchman for leaded glass is a flat piece of came without a heart that covers the crack on one or both sides of the glass and tucks under the flange where the crack begins or ends. If possible, solder the came ends.

If a piece of glass is so fractured that the use of a Dutchman is insufficient, the piece will have to be removed, but not before it is taped together with strong masking tape. This precaution is most important in the case of a painted piece to assure that the lines of the new piece of glass will coincide with the rest of the window. (Use transparent tape on painted glass.) The pattern for the new piece of glass is made from the broken piece, taped together.

To remove the cracked, taped piece from the rest of the window, make diagonal cuts in the corners of the came joints and pry up the flanges. In the case of half-round came (which precludes prying), sufficient flange will have to be cut away to enable removal of the piece and replacement with the new piece. Cut away only as much flange as is necessary. You will have to solder on a new flange, and vertical soldering is a chore at best. A soldering iron can be tried, but a soldering gun is a better choice.

It is especially important to clean the lead before soldering. Use a small wire brush and steel wool. Under the circumstances, a plumber's candle is a more practical flux than liquid oleic acid.

If not enough of the piece can be salvaged for taping, make a pattern by fitting cardboard into the opening. Keep fragments of the piece for color and install plain glass temporarily. Make a tracing of the broken area and the adjoining pieces to indicate the lines, and so on, needed for replacement.

For a copper foil piece, remove as much solder as possible with a soldering iron, front and back (solder follows a hot iron). Bend foil edges and remove damaged piece; replace with a new one, or rewrap fragments and replace. Sometimes adhesive-backed foil can be applied over a crack and a bead carefully soldered on.

Care and delicate handling are required when fitting glass into place so as not to fracture older neighboring pieces.

INSTALLATION FOR FLAT GLASS PANEL

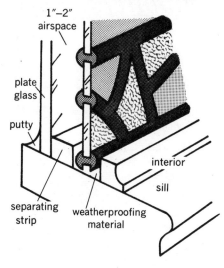

INSTALLATION FOR SLAB GLASS PANEL

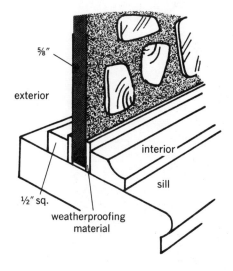

# *Suppliers*

## General

Allcraft Tool & Supply Co.
215 Park Ave.
Hicksville, N.Y. 11801

Arts & Crafts Colony
4132 N. Tamiami Trail
Sarasota, Fla. 33580

Bergen Arts & Crafts
Box 381
Marblehead, Mass. 01945

S. Camlott
520 Hollywood Ave.
Salt Lake City, Utah 84105

Glass Masters Guild
52 Carmine St.
New York, N.Y. 10014

Kraft Korner
5864 Mayfield Rd.
Cleveland, Ohio 44124

Sax Arts & Crafts
207 N. Milwaukee St.
Milwaukee, Wis. 53202

Saylescrafts, Inc.
171 Main St.
Nyack, N.Y. 10960

Whittemore-Durgin
803 Washington Ave.
Hanover, Mass. 02339

## Glass

S. A. Bendheim Co., Inc.
122 Hudson Ave.
New York, N.Y. 10013

Bienenfeld Industries, Inc.
1541 Covert St.
Brooklyn, N.Y. 11227

Blenko Glass Co.
Milton, W.Va. 25541

Kokomo Opalescent Glass Co.
Kokomo, Ind. 46901

The Paul Wissmach Glass Co.
Paden City, W. Va. 26159

## Lead Came and Solder

Gardiner Metal Co.
4820 S. Campbell Ave.
Chicago, Ill. 60632

National Lead Co.
1050 State St.
Perth Amboy, N.J. 08861

White Metal Rolling &
    Stamping Corp.
80 Moultrie St.
Brooklyn, N.Y. 11222

## Copper Foil and Wire

Conklin Brass & Copper Co., Inc.
324 W. 23rd St.
New York, N.Y. 10011

Paragon Industries, Inc.
Box 10133
Dallas, Tex. 75207

## Cutting and Glazing Tools

Concord Co.
421 Hunts Point Ave.
Bronx, N.Y. 10474

Glazier Hardware Co.
1689 First Ave.
New York, N.Y. 10028

Henry Westpfal & Co., Inc.
4 E. 32nd St.
New York, N.Y. 10016

## Soldering Irons

Hexacon Electric Co.
161 W. Clay Ave.
Roselle Park, N.J. 07204

Ungar
Division of Eldon Industries, Inc.
Compton, Calif. 90220

## Flux and Patina

City Chemical Corp.
132-4 W. 22nd St.
New York, N.Y. 10011

## Epoxy

Benesco
40 N. Rock Hill Rd.
St. Louis, Mo. 63119

H.C.H. Chemicals
2055 W. Gaylord St.
Long Beach, Calif. 90813

H & M Plastics
129 S. 2nd Ave.
Philadelphia, Pa. 19106

Polyproducts Corps.
Dept. 52
13810 Nelson Ave.
Detroit, Mich. 48227

Resins Research Co.
1989 Bayberry Rd.
Huntingdon Valley, Pa. 19006

## Paints (Oxides)

American Art Clay Co.
4717 W. 16th
Indianapolis, Ind. 46222

J & H Art Glass Supply
522 Madison
Fredonia, Kan. 66736

L. Reusche & Co.
2-6 Lister Ave.
Newark, N.J. 07105

Stewart Clay Co., Inc.
133 Mulberry St.
New York, N.Y. 10013

## Kilns

Kress Kilns
323 W. Maple Ave.
Monrovia, Calif. 91016

Paragon Industries, Inc.
Box 10133
Dallas, Tex. 75207

Wilt Industries
860 Albany-Shaker Rd.
Latham, N.Y. 12110

# *For Further Reading*

## BOOKS

Albers, Josef, *INTERACTION OF COLOR,* Yale University Press, New Haven, Conn., 1971.

Anderson, Harriette, *KILN-FIRED GLASS,* Chilton Book Co., Philadelphia, Pa., 1970.

Armitage, E. Liddall, *STAINED GLASS, History, Technology, and Practice,* Charles T. Branford Co., Newton, Mass., 1959.

Connick, Charles J., *ADVENTURES IN LIGHT & COLOR,* Random House, New York, N.Y., 1937.

Duval, Jean-Jacques, *WORKING WITH STAINED GLASS,* Thomas Y. Crowell Co., New York, N.Y. 1972.

Hess, Thomas B., and Ashbery, John, *LIGHT IN ART, from Aten to Laser,* Art News Annual XXXV, The Macmillan Co., New York, N.Y., 1970.

Kinney, Kay, *GLASS CRAFT,* Chilton Book Co., Philadelphia, Pa., 1962.

Mollica, Peter, *STAINED GLASS PRIMER,* Mollica Stained Glass Press, Berkeley, Calif., 1971.

Reyntiens, Patrick, *THE TECHNIQUE OF STAINED GLASS,* Watson-Guptill Publications, New York, N.Y., 1967.

Smith, Charles N., *STUDENT HANDBOOK OF COLOR,* Van Nostrand-Reinhold, New York, N.Y., 1965.

Sowers, Robert W., *THE LOST ART, A Survey of 1000 Years of Stained Glass,* George Wittenborn, Inc., New York, N.Y., 1954.

—— *STAINED GLASS, An Architectural Art,* Universe Books, New York, N.Y., 1965.

Wood, Paul W., *STAINED GLASS CRAFTING,* Sterling Publ. Co., Inc., New York, N.Y., 1967.


## PERIODICALS

*CRAFT HORIZONS,* published bimonthly by the American Crafts Council, 44 W. 53rd St., New York, N.Y. 10019.

*GLASS ART MAGAZINE,* published bimonthly. Glass Art Magazine, P.O. Box 7527, Oakland, Calif. 94601.

*STAINED GLASS,* published bimonthly by The Stained Glass Association of America, 1125 Wilmington Ave., St. Louis, Mo. 63111.


## BOOK SERVICES

*Craft & Hobby Book Service,* P.O. Box 626, Pacific Grove, Calif. 93950.

*Museum Books, Inc.,* 48 E. 43rd St., New York, N.Y. 10017.

*The Unicorn Books for Craftsmen,* P.O. Box 645, Rockville, Md. 20851.

Leaded door panel incorporating beveled plate glass and rondels blown by the designers, Jamie Carpenter and Dale Chihuly. Collection, The Corning Museum of Glass, Corning, N.Y.

# Schools & Workshops

The following is a partial list of schools and workshops that offer instruction in stained glass. For further information, write to the school or workshop direct.

Mountain View Branch
of Foothills Vo-Tech School
P.O. Box 359
Ozark Folk Center
Mountain View, **Ark.** 72560

Augustine Glass Works
711 Colorado Ave.
Santa Monica, **Calif.** 90401

California State Univ.,
San Diego
5402 College Ave.
San Diego, **Calif.** 92115

College of Marin
Kentfield, **Calif.** 94904

The de Young Museum
Art School
Golden Gate Park
San Francisco, **Calif.** 94118

El Camino College
16007 Crenshaw Blvd.
Torrance, **Calif.** 90506

Mendocino Art Center
Mendocino, **Calif.** 95460

Mollica Stained Glass
1940 Bonita Ave.
Berkeley, **Calif.** 94704

Nervo Studios
2027 7th St.
Berkeley, **Calif.** 94710

San Francisco Art Institute
800 Chestnut
San Francisco, **Calif.** 94133

Univ. of California,
Los Angeles
1300 Dickson Art Center
Los Angeles, **Calif.** 90024

Young, Joseph
Art in Architecture
Mosaic Workshop
1434 S. Spaulding Ave.
Los Angeles, **Calif.** 90019

Brookfield Craft Center, Inc.
Route 25
Brookfield, **Conn.** 06804

Smithsonian Institution
Smithsonian Associates
Washington, **D.C.** 20560

Haystack School of Crafts
Deer Isle, **Me.** 04627

Boston Center
for Adult Education
5 Commonwealth Ave.
Boston, **Mass.** 02116

Cambridge Center
for Adult Education
42 Brattle St.
Cambridge, **Mass.** 02138

Decordova Museum
Sandy Pond Rd.
Lincoln, **Mass.** 01773

The Old Schwamb Mill
17 Mill Lane at 29 Lowell
Arlington, **Mass.** 02174

School of the Museum
of Fine Arts
230 The Fenway
Boston, **Mass.** 02115

School of Associated Arts
344 Summit Ave.
St. Paul, **Minn.** 55102

College of Great Falls
1301 20th St. South
Great Falls, **Mont.** 59401

Franklin Pierce College
Rindge, **N.H.** 03461

Artist & Craftsman Guild
17 Eastman St.
Cranford, **N.J.** 07016

The Salem Craftsmen's
Guild
1042 Salem Road
Union, **N.J.** 07083

Wiss Studio & Craft
Workshop
161 Culberson Rd.
Basking Ridge, **N.J.** 07920

Bronx Community College
120 E. 184th St.
Bronx, **N.Y.** 10468

Brooklyn Museum
Art School
188 Eastern Pkwy.
Brooklyn, **N.Y.** 11238

Craft Student League
West Side YWCA
840 8th Ave.
New York, **N.Y.** 10019

Durham Studios, Inc.
115 E. 18th St.
New York, **N.Y.** 10003

Jean-Jacques Duval
Workshop
58 W. 15th St.
New York, **N.Y.** 10011

The New School
66 West 12th St.
New York, **N.Y.** 10011

The Riverside Church
Arts & Crafts Program
490 Riverside Drive
New York, **N.Y.** 10027

Rockland Ctr. for the Arts
27 Old Greenbush Rd.
West Nyack, **N.Y.** 10994

Stained Glass Workshop
136 Henry St.
New York, **N.Y.** 10002

Syracuse University
Lowe Art Center
Syracuse, **N.Y.** 13210

92nd Street YM-YWHA
1395 Lexington Ave.
New York, **N.Y.** 10028

Gaston College
New Dallas Highway
Dallas, **N.C.** 28034

Penland School of Crafts
Penland, **N.C.** 28765

Riverbend Art Center
142 River Bend Dr.
Dayton, **Ohio** 45405

Corvallis Arts Center
700 S.W. Madison
Corvallis, **Ore.** 97330

Eastern Oregon College
8th & K Ave.
La Grande, **Ore.** 97850

Maude Kerns Art Center
1910 E. 15th
Eugene, **Ore.** 97403

The Arts & Crafts Center
of Pittsburgh
Fifth and Shady Aves.
Pittsburgh, **Pa.** 15232

East Stroudsburg State Coll.
East Stroudsburg, **Pa.** 18301

Southern Craft Center
Creative Art School
300 Augusta
San Antonio, **Tex.** 78205

Artistic Glass
315 South 2100, E.
Salt Lake City, **Utah** 84115

Spokane Falls Community Coll.
Fort Wright Campus
Spokane, **Wash.** 99204

Oglebay Institute
841½ National Rd.
Wheeling, **W. Va.** 26003

Mount Mary College
2900 Menomonee River Pkwy.
Milwaukee, **Wis.** 53222

ABCDEF